A
REPORT
TO THE
FORD
FOUNDATION

Hispanic Theater in the United States and Puerto Rico

by Joanne Pottlitzer

D1402174

Ford Foundation
New York

One of a series of reports on activities supported
by the Ford Foundation. A complete list of
publications may be obtained from the
Ford Foundation, Office of Reports.
320 East 43 Street, New York, N.Y. 10017.

**Library of Congress Cataloging-in-
Publication Data**
Pottlitzer, Joanne.
   Hispanic theater in the United States
and Puerto Rico.

   1. Hispanic American theater—United States.
2. Hispanic American theater—Puerto Rico.
I. Ford Foundation. II. Title.
PN2270.H57P68   1988   792'.08968073
88-21220   ISBN 0-916584-33-X

Contents

Preface

In 1984, as part of its effort to support the richness and diversity of the arts in the United States, the Foundation began an initiative in Hispanic theater. In keeping with the Foundation's commitment to cultural pluralism, the initiative aimed to further the development of a vigorous art form with a wide range of styles and a growing audience. Its efforts encompassed strengthening Hispanic theater institutions, offering increased opportunities to Hispanic theater artists, and fostering touring and networking activities. To date the Foundation has expended $3.4 million on these activities.

This report on Hispanic theater in the United States was originally prepared to acquaint the Foundation with the scope of Hispanic theater activity and to place it in a broader historical and cultural context. In the course of her two-year research throughout the country in 1984-85, Joanne Pottlitzer uncovered so much interesting material, both historical and current, that we decided to make the report available to a wider audience.

Joanne Pottlitzer has been immersed in Hispanic theater in Latin America and the United States for over two decades. She has worked as a director, translated plays, and produced and presented major Latin American plays and companies in this country. In the course of this study Ms. Pottlitzer surveyed some 150 institutions and interviewed more than 200 people connected with Hispanic theater. Her report was updated in 1987 so that the institutional information would be as current as possible. Nonetheless, the report does not claim to be inclusive. The field it covers is volatile—new theater groups come into existence, others disappear, and leadership changes.

The report has been prepared for publication by Nina Kressner Cobb, a writer, editor, and historian who works as a consultant with several foundations. As editor, Ms. Cobb worked intensively with Ms. Pottlitzer and made an important contribution to the completion of what we believe to be a unique document.

The report discusses Hispanic theater within its complex cultural context. Chapters Two and Three present a brief history of Hispanic theater activity throughout the northern hemisphere—emphasizing regional differences and the variety of genres. Chapter Four surveys current theater activity in the United States. Chapter Five presents recommendations for increasing the stability and fostering the growth of this rich art form.

We believe this publication will be valuable to those engaged in creating, producing, presenting, or funding the theater in the United States as well as to those with a special interest in Hispanic culture and its diverse manifestations.

Susan V. Berresford
Vice-President
U.S. and International Affairs Programs
Ford Foundation

1. Historical Context:
Diversity of Culture

Theater is a reflection of the society that creates it and Hispanic theater is no exception. Hispanic theater in the United States, which dates to the 16th century, is as diverse as the people it portrays. According to 1986 and 1987 census data, Hispanics constitute more than 10 percent of the total U.S. population.[1] They include 18.7 million Mexican Americans, Cubans, Puerto Ricans, Dominicans, Central and South Americans in the fifty states and 3.3 million Puerto Ricans living in Puerto Rico. Mexican Americans make up 60 percent of the U.S. mainland Hispanic population; Puerto Ricans 14 percent; and Cubans 6 percent; the remaining 20 percent are from other parts of Latin America and the Caribbean.

The diverse meanings of the word Hispanic reflect a heterogeneity that the word obscures. In New Mexico, Hispanic refers only to the descendants of the Spaniards who settled there in the 16th century. In the East, Hispanic is the generic term for people with Spanish surnames, although some consider Hispanic to be an elitist term. Therefore, many with Spanish surnames prefer Latino to Hispanic as the generic term of identification.

The words Chicano and Mexican American also evoke different connotations. The term Chicano has been in common usage in California and the Southwest for generations; some believe it derives from the word *Mexicano*. It frequently connotes political activism among Mexican Americans.

Hispanics derive from countries in the Americas where Spanish is the dominant language and Roman Catholicism the major religion. This includes people of African descent from the Dominican Republic and Cuba, those of American-Indian background from Mexico and Central America, and others of European roots from Chile and Argentina.

The preponderance of Hispanics living in the United States cannot trace their ancestors directly to Spain. Rather, most are descendants of different cultures, be they mestizo (Spanish and Indian); mulatto (African and Spanish); or a combination of Spanish, Indian, and African. Other Hispanics have Chinese, Lebanese, English, and European heritages, but their cultural identity remains Latino/Hispanic.

Though Hispanic theater in the United States represents all of these diverse cultures, the majority of its artists are of Mexican, Puerto Rican, Cuban, and more recently, Central American backgrounds. The following brief description of their migratory histories will provide a context for understanding both the theatrical expression and the isolation found among Hispanic theaters.

The Mexican presence in the United States is the longest and most complex of all the Hispanic groups, dating back to pre-Columbian times. After the Mexican War of Independence against Spain (1810-1821), the new republic of Mexico encompassed what is now the entire Southwest and West Coast of the United States up to the northern borders of California, Nevada, and Utah. That land, which comprised half of the Mexican nation and is now more than one-third of the continental United States, was lost under the terms of the Guadalupe-Hidalgo Treaty in 1848 after Mexico's defeat in the Mexican-American War. So the first Hispanics in the United States were not immigrants. "We did not, in fact, come to the United States at all," says Luis Valdez, founder of El Teatro Campesino in California. "The United States came to us."[2]

For almost a century, Mexicans crossed the border at will because the boundary established by the treaty was not enforced by either side. The largest migration took place as a result of the Mexican Revolution (1910-1921), when an estimated one million Mexicans of varied economic backgrounds crossed into the United States. The first to come were those escaping the revolution; others came after World War I broke out, when the American economy expanded and additional labor was needed. (From the West Coast to Appalachia, Mexicans were hired as field hands, miners, and factory workers.) By 1930 Chicago had become the largest Spanish-speaking area in the United States outside of the Southwest.

During the Depression of the 1930s, more than 500,000 Mexicans, approximately half of them American-born, were sent back to Mexico by federal order; this deprived the Southwest of 10 percent of its Mexican American population and depleted the Midwest Mexican population by one-half.[3] When World War II created new labor needs, the United States government again allowed Mexicans to enter the United States, to work on a temporary basis under the *bracero,* or "hired-hand" program, which at its height attracted some 400,000 workers annually.[4] Many Mexicans continued to cross the border illegally in search of work and, in 1954, when legal action was taken against them, more than one million Mexicans were deported. These back-and-forth immigration policies have not enhanced trust in the United States government or facilitated the continuity and development of Mexican American communities.

In 1970, 50 percent of all Mexican Americans were third generation or more.[5] Old Spanish families in New Mexico, third-generation Mexican American businessmen and politicians in Texas, second-generation youths in the barrios of Los Angeles, and first-generation laborers throughout the United States are part of the complex culture created by this long history of Mexican migration.

Puerto Rican and Cuban migration to the United States began in the latter part of the 19th century. As Spanish political repression of these Caribbean colonies increased, immigrants fled northward to open businesses and organize independence movements in several U.S. cities. Puerto Rican merchants and political exiles went to Philadelphia and New York. Cubans migrated to Florida, settling in Key West and Tampa.[6] Among the first were cigar manufacturers; they created jobs for many of their compatriots who continued to flow into Florida. The Key West community became a strong financial supporter of the liberation of Cuba from Spain. Since the Spanish-American War of 1898, the United States has also served as a home for Cuban political and artistic dissidents. In the 1930s exiles from the Machado dictatorship fled to Miami and New York, a process that was repeated twenty years later under the Batista regime. The Cuban population of the United States swelled after the Castro Revolution of 1959. The Cuban population of Miami before Fidel Castro's rise to power was 20,000. It is now over one-half million.[7]

Puerto Ricans were granted U.S. citizenship in 1917, but they cannot vote in national elections. Their citizenship has facilitated movement to and from the United States, but has also caused political controversy among Puerto Ricans, even after the island obtained commonwealth status in 1953. Puerto Rican migration to the United States expanded greatly after World War II, when large groups of working-class people poured into New York City. Between 1940 and 1950, the Puerto Rican population in the United States rose from 70,000 to more than

300,000 and centered in New York. During the next three decades, migration accelerated even more and spilled over into New Jersey, Pennsylvania, and Illinois. Today Puerto Ricans constitute the second largest Hispanic population in the United States after Mexican Americans.

Immigrants from Central and South America, more scattered throughout the United States than other Hispanic groups and covering a broader economic range, had come here primarily for economic reasons until the last decade when political turmoil sparked considerable migration. Central Americans by the hundreds of thousands have come to the United States in search of refuge and a new life. At least 1.5 million immigrants from El Salvador alone are said to be living in the United States. Most have arrived here since 1980.

NOTES

1. *Hispanic Population in the United States: March 1986 and March 1987.* (Advance Report. Series P20 #416. August 1987) U.S. Bureau of the Census. Department of Commerce, pp. 2, 5. *Estimates Report of the Population of Puerto Rico and the Outlying Areas: 1980-1986* (#P25-1009, 1986) U.S. Bureau of the Census Estimates Reports, p. 7.

2. Jorge A. Huerta, *Chicano Theatre: Themes and Forms,* Ypsilanti, Michigan: Bilingual Press/Editorial Bilingue, 1982, p. 4.

3. Matt S. Meier and Feliciano Rivera, *The Chicanos,* New York: Hill and Wang, 1972, pp. 160-163.

4. William Diaz, *Hispanics: Challenges and Opportunities,* A Ford Foundation working paper, New York, 1984, p. 120.

5. *Ibid.,* p.11.

6. As a result of the Treaty of Paris (1783), the Florida territory, which had been ceded to Britian twenty years earlier and became her fourteenth and fifteenth American colonies, was returned to Spain. Spain sold the territory to the United States in 1821.

7. Jan Knippers Black, Howard I. Blustein, J. David Edwards, Kathryn Therese Johnson, David S. McMorris, *Area Handbook for Cuba,* Washington D.C.: Foreign Area Studies of the American University, 1976, p. 35.

2. A Brief History of Hispanic Theater in the United States and Puerto Rico: 1865-1965

THE UNITED STATES

Hispanic theater has a long and varied tradition in the United States. The first play staged in what is now the United States, *Los moros y los cristianos,* was produced in 1598 by Spanish colonizers belonging to Juan de Oñate's expedition to Nuevo Mexico. It was performed near San Juan Pueblo in the area of Santa Fe. The long history of Spanish dramaturgy and its tradition of *autosacramentales* performed on religious holidays, coupled with the centrality of religious ritual and dramatic spectacle in Mexican and Central American Indian life, made theater and performance a natural part of Mexican culture.

Professional Mexican theater troupes that had toured the northern Mexican provinces before they were ceded to the United States had become resident companies in Los Angeles and San Francisco by the 1860s. They presented Spanish melodramas and *zarzuelas* (operettas) and an occasional Mexican or Cuban play. *Zarzuelas* and melodramas dominated the stage until the 1920s, but theater was also used for political ends. One of the most important companies based in San Francisco, La Familia Estrella, held frequent performances to raise money for the Republican cause in Mexico during the French intervention there (1862-1867). More often, plays were written to raise funds for people who, from the perspective of the community, were wrongly accused of crimes.[1] For example, Gregorio Cortez, a young Mexican imprisoned unjustly for killing a sheriff who had trespassed on his land, was memorialized first in a *corrido* (ballad) at the turn of the century and recently in a film entitled *The Corrido of Gregorio Cortez,* starring James Edward Olmos.

By the turn of the 19th century, touring circuits for Mexican companies and artists had been established all along the Mexican border in Texas, New Mexico, and Arizona; and along the California coast from San Diego to San Francisco. The influx of Mexicans after the Mexican Revolution brought even more artists to the

United States and created a greater demand for Spanish-language theater. Coast-to-coast touring circuits were developed from New York to Philadelphia, Cleveland, Chicago, and on to Los Angeles. Some artists stayed in the United States and started their own companies. Among the most celebrated was the legendary actress Virginia Fabregas, who brought new plays from Mexico and encouraged writers in the United States.

Theater, like the Church and political organizations, was established in all Mexican immigrant cities and barrios. The Teatro Carmen, built by the Mexican community of Tucson in 1915 to house traveling troupes, played an important role in the growth of Hispanic theater. At that time, Tucson had a population of about fifteen thousand, half of whom were Mexican. Owners of mines and ranches and political exiles from the 1910 Revolution gave money and encouragement to build the 1400-seat house in response to a large demand for theater by the city's middle-class Mexicans.[2]

Nicolas Kanellos noted the historically close relationship between theater and the Hispanic community in his book on Hispanic theater in the United States: ". . . the Hispanic stage served to reinforce the sense of community by bringing all Spanish-speakers together in a cultural act: the preservation of the culture in a foreign environment and for resistance against the influence of the dominant society."[3] Local groups often dramatized the political and social dilemmas of Mexican Americans and new immigrants. In the early 1920s, Los Angeles became a center for Mexican American playwrights who wrote for small, community-based theaters.

Another genre of Mexican theatrical tradition that toured small border towns and rural areas in the Southwest from the turn of the century to the 1920s was the *carpa* (tent) teatro. *Carpa* troupes were composed largely of families or extended families. La Carpa Garcia, one of the best-known troupes, was based in San Antonio and performed throughout the Southwest from 1914 until the late 1940s. Rooted in circus and clowning techniques, *carpa* teatros were known for their biting humor, social and political satire, and music. The aesthetic of these *carpa* teatros was called "rascuachism," a view of the world from the perspective of the downtrodden or outsider. The *rascuachi* character always had a spirit of irreverence, "a carnivalesque, topsy-turvy vision where authority and decorum served as targets for subversion."[4]

Even more than melodramas and *zarzuelas, carpas* helped to establish a new sense of identity for the Mexican American in the Southwest. They reached more people and appealed to their sense of humor while revealing the struggle of their daily lives. Early *carpa* teatros satirized Mexican Americans who began to become Americanized, a process called *agringamiento.* Many jokes were based on such linguistic plays on words as double entendres, with sexual overtones and mistakes in pronunciation of both English and Spanish words. The central figure in these shows was the *pelado,* which means "naked" in Spanish, a Mexican everyman who is both irreverent and sympathetic—the prototype for the Cantinflas character and similar to Charlie Chaplin's Little Tramp. The *pelado's* comic routines were "a sounding board for the culture conflict that Mexican Americans felt in language usage, assimilation to American tastes and life style, discrimination in the United States, and *pocho* [a pejorative slang for a Mexican born in the United States] status in Mexico. . . . the *pelado* became a precursor in defining a bilingual, bicultural sensibility."[5]

In the 1920s *tandas de variedad* (variety shows), a form of popular theater that openly used Anglo vaudevillian techniques and styles, incorporated aspects of both cultures and, as such, appealed to a younger generation—the sons and daughters of the refugees of the Mexican Revolution and the sons and daughters of the long-established *tejanos, manitos,* and *californios.*[6] According to Tomas Ybarra-Frausto,

> The *teatro de revista* [revues] played a crucial role in projecting from the stage the popular base of an emerging national culture. The younger generation from both groups was the one which most creatively responded to the new reality in the assumption of a bi-sensibility that transformed and re-contextualized cultural elements for both cultures in a new synthesis.[7]

Together the *carpas* and *tandas de variedad* created an alternative vaudeville circuit in the United States that lasted until the 1950s, three decades longer than Anglo-American vaudeville. The style and content of these genres formed the basis for the contemporary Chicano theater that emerged in the mid-1960s. Chicano theater continues to bridge the two cultures.

Spanish-language theater in the United States reached its high point in the 1920s. In Los Angeles and San Antonio, the largest centers of Hispanic theater

in the West, more than twenty theaters presented Spanish melodramas, *zarzuelas,*
local plays, and *tandas de revistas.* Touring companies took shows on regional and
national circuits, and *carpa* teatros played smaller towns and rural circuits
throughout the Southwest. Even Chicago, with recent migrants from the Southwest
and Mexico, contained at least five community theater groups. The strongest of
these, the Cuadro Dramatico del Circulo de Obreros Catolicos San Jose, was
founded in 1925. Like other Mexican American theater groups, the Cuadro
Dramatico had strong community involvement, instilling migrants and immigrants
with dignity and pride in their cultural heritage; it also helped raise funds to build
Our Lady of Guadalupe Church in the Mexican American community of East
Chicago. Under the direction of J. Jesus Cabrera, the Cuadro Dramatico
performed traditional plays instead of *carpas* or *tandas de variedad.*

New York and Tampa were the eastern centers of the Hispanic theater boom
of the 1920s. Spanish-language theater had been introduced in both cities by
touring companies from Spain and Cuba at the turn of the century. Mexican and
Argentine troupes also visited New York. By the 1920s both cities boasted stable,
professional theater communities made up of local and visiting artists. Although
their repertoires would occasionally include a new play about the lives of Hispanic
immigrants, they generally presented *zarzuelas,* established plays by Calderon de la
Barca and Lope de Vega, and musical revues. The first professional resident
theater company in New York, La Compania de Teatro Español, which was
founded in 1921, catered to middle-class Spaniards and Cubans who made up over
50 percent of New York's Hispanic population at that time.

Hispanics and their theater venues were scattered throughout the city in
neighborhood clusters that later became known as Hispanic areas, such as East
Harlem and the Lower East Side. But "there were (also) Galicians and Basques
living on Cherry Street . . . and there were Andalucians living in Brooklyn."[8] The
most popular theaters were the Park Palace on 110th Street and Fifth Avenue and
the Apollo Theatre on 125th Street in Harlem.

The New York Hispanic theater movement of the 1920s had its stars just as
the Mexican American movement did. One of the most famous was the Spanish
actress Maria Reid who played the Spanish circuit in New York, formed her own
company, and "crossed over" to play on Broadway. In the early 1950s Reid played

in a production of Jane Bowles's *In the Summer House* under the direction of Jose Quintero.

The Depression years, the Spanish Civil War, and World War II took their toll on Hispanic theater throughout the country. Hispanic theater virtually came to an end in Tampa until a WPA Federal Theatre program revived it in the late 1930s with a Spanish-language theater project. That project provided roots for the Spanish Lyric Theatre, founded in Tampa in 1959. In New York, Hispanic theaters began to neglect legitimate plays and musicals to concentrate on variety shows. In addition, the large Puerto Rican migration which began in the late 1930s and boomed in the late 1940s and 1950s heightened demand for such entertainment. The Puerto Rican who came to New York was, for the most part, of rural and working-class background with little theatrical tradition. The rhythms heard at the Park Palace and other theaters became more Puerto Rican each year. In the 1940s musical revues dominated the theater scene, although Garcia Lorca's plays could be found at Columbia University and Barnard College where they were presented by refugees of the Spanish Civil War who were on the faculty.

Legitimate theater reappeared among the Hispanic communities in New York and Chicago in the mid-1950s. In 1954 a young Puerto Rican director Roberto Rodriguez produced a new Puerto Rican play, *La Carreta* (*The Oxcart*) by the then-unknown Rene Marques. The drama traced a rural Puerto Rican family as it moved to the slums of urban San Juan and then to New York in search of a better life. The play, which opened in Spanish at the Church of San Sebastian on 24th Street between First and Second Avenues, was a success. As a result, Rodriguez and Miriam Colon, one of the actresses and an important figure in Hispanic theater today, founded the first Hispanic theater group in New York with its own theater, El Circulo Dramatico.[9] Located on Sixth Avenue between 43rd and 44th Streets, the sixty-seat house opened in 1956 with a Cuban play. In 1958 the Fire Department closed the theater. Ironically, the Puerto Rican Traveling Theatre, which Colon founded in 1967, now has its permanent home in a renovated New York firehouse.

The Hispanic community of the Chicago area lost its small community theaters along with half of its population, with the mass deportation of Mexicans and Mexican Americans during the Depression. Theater activity was revived in the

1950s when Puerto Ricans who had migrated to the Midwest in the 1940s began to express themselves theatrically, usually through church groups and mutual aid societies, as Mexicans had done before them. Little is known about either Mexican or Puerto Rican theater in the Chicago area during that period, except that they were community-based and their activity was related to religious holidays.

The Depression years and the deportation of Mexicans did not wipe out the *tandas de variedad*, which had strong popular support, on the West Coast or in the Southwest. On the contrary, the *tandas* became more explicitly political. When 500,000 Mexican American servicemen went overseas to fight in World War II, many *corridos* depicting their fate appeared in the variety shows. The *pachuco* replaced the *pelado* as a symbol of cultural conflict, Mexican American rebelliousness, and resistance in the *tandas de variedad*. Whereas the *pelado* communicated a feeling of naivete and subservience coupled with cleverness and wit, the *pachuco* displayed a slick urban arrogance and flamboyance.

The growing popularity of movies and the advent of television were disastrous for *tandas* and *carpas*, which died out in the 1950s. The political turmoil of the 1960s and the struggle of the Chicano farmworkers in California served as midwife to the birth of El Teatro Campesino under the leadership of Luis Valdez in 1965.

PUERTO RICO

Although Puerto Rico has been bound legally to the United States since 1898 and as a Commonwealth since 1953, it is culturally closer in many respects to Latin America. Theater of consequence did not appear there until the middle of the 19th century. The Taino-Arawak Indians who inhabited the island when Ponce de Leon colonized it in 1504 did not have a cultural life comparable to the more advanced civilizations of Mexico, Guatemala, or the Andean region of South America. After the Spanish conquest, Church and military censorship curtailed theater activity in Puerto Rico well into the 19th century.

The first municipal theater, built in San Juan in 1832, was served by touring companies from abroad. Called the Teatro Tapia, after Alejandro Tapia y Rivera, considered Puerto Rico's first national playwright, it still stands and is in constant use. Tapia's plays, which were often subjected to censorship, were exceptional in their criticisms of slavery and the Spanish monarchy. The *costumbrista,* or "slice-of-life," style also found its way into 19th-century theater with the *jibaro* (the Puerto Rican campesino) and blacks as central characters. Women wrote plays during that period, setting a precedent for the active role women now play in Puerto Rican theater.

During the first several decades after the United States replaced Spain as the dominant power in Puerto Rican politics and economic life, plays began to dramatize that political situation. Some were socialist in theme and took up the cause of the proletariat; some questioned the values of the middle class; others reflected the current political climate and the island's history. Two plays written in this period stand out: *El Grito de Lares* (*The Cry of Lares*) (1914) by the national poet Luis Llorens Torres and *Juan Ponce De Leon* (1929) by Carlos Carreras and Jose Ramirez Santibañez.[10] Both were historical romances protesting Spanish domination, but were clearly directed against American control.

Since the late 1940s the quest for national identity has been a dominant theme of Puerto Rican plays. Luis Rafael Sanchez, Puerto Rico's most notable contemporary playwright, commented on that tradition in an interview with Gloria Waldman:

> Puerto Rican theater has been essentially nationalistic and so it must be, because in Puerto Rico there is a political problem which has not been resolved. Because a fundamental part of our mentality is separatist, "independentist," the theme which is always examined theatrically is that of the disappearance of our personality as a people—that is, [our] transculturation, the problem of Puerto Ricans in New York as an oppressed minority, the participation of Puerto Ricans in conflicts which tie them to the United States.[11]

The year 1940 was a turning point in Puerto Rico's political and theatrical history. That year marked the election to the Puerto Rican Senate of Luis Muñoz Marin, who was to become the island's first Puerto Rican governor in 1948, thirty-one years after Puerto Ricans were granted United States citizenship. It was also in 1940 that the Areyto Drama Society was founded by a group of young playwrights inspired by Emilio S. Belaval, himself a playwright and an attorney. Belaval called for the creation of a theater using national themes, actors, scenery, ideas, and aesthetics. The name Areyto was chosen because it was the name of a ritual pageant of music, dance, and pantomime performed by the Taino Indians who originally inhabited the island. Areyto lasted only one year, but it launched Puerto Rico's contemporary theater movement.

During its one season, with the vision of Belaval and the directorial and production experience of Leopoldo Santiago Lavandero, who trained at the Yale School of Drama, Areyto produced works by Manuel Mendez Ballester, Luis Rechani Agrait, Martha Lomar, and Fernando Sierra Berdecia. Areyto laid the groundwork for subsequent generations of playwrights, including Rene Marques, Francisco Arrivi, Enrique Laguerre, Edmundo Rivera Alvarez, Gerard Paul Marin, Myrna Casas, and Luis Rafael Sanchez.

The momentum toward the development of a national theater was interrupted when the production of Puerto Rican plays at the University of Puerto Rico was banned by the government in 1944. The ban was imposed following a production of Enrique Laguerre's *La Resentida* (*The Bitter Woman*), which dramatized the political unrest in Puerto Rico against Spain, specifically the peasant unrest against Spanish landowners in 1898. The play's reference to the current political situation in Puerto Rico did not go unnoticed. After 10,000 people saw and praised the production, the ban on Puerto Rican plays was instituted against the wishes of Lavandero, then head of the university's drama department. The ban was not lifted until 1956 with the production of a play by Francisco Arrivi.

The Experimental Theatre of the 110-year-old cultural center Ateneo Puertorriqueño was established in 1951 under the leadership of Jose Lacomba and playwright Rene Marques. In 1955 the Instituto de Cultura Puertorriqueña was founded with Francisco Arrivi at the helm of the theater department. Both institutions launched annual national theater festivals to encourage Puerto Rican playwrights. The first festival sponsored by the instituto, in 1958, included Francisco Arrivi's *Vejigantes*, an examination of racial prejudice, and *Los Soles Truncos* (*Fanlights*), Rene Marques's dramatization of industrialization's disruption of traditional social values. The Instituto de Cultura continues to hold festivals each year, as does the Ateneo, though they are less significant for developing new plays than they were in their first two decades.

The plays of Arrivi and Marques dominated the Puerto Rican stage through the 1950s and into the 1960s. Their plays have Puerto Rican themes and styles that tend toward naturalism or social realism. In addition to *Los Soles Truncos*,

Marques's best-known work is *La Carreta*. Both plays have achieved the status of classics and have been successfully produced in New York and in other parts of the United States. Arrivi has also made a strong contribution to Puerto Rican theater through his untiring promotion of national writers and groups and his prolific and complete documentation of the history of Puerto Rican theater. The 1986 festival of the Instituto de Cultura Puertorriqueña was dedicated to plays by Arrivi, and a revival of his *Vejigantes* opened the event.

Luis Rafael Sanchez, who led a new generation of playwrights, began writing realistic plays in the 1950s. Even then, his use of dense poetic language set him apart from others of his generation. His later use of farce, expressionism, and symbolism broke new stylistic ground for the next generation. In the early 1960s Myrna Casas was writing absurdist plays. Both Casas and Sanchez were revolutionaries for their departures in style, but perhaps even more for the themes they chose. Sanchez explored radical Marxist political positions; Casas, new familial and sexual roles. In 1963 Casas co-founded Producciones Cisne, which produces her plays and translations of U.S. and European works.

The 1960s also saw the establishment of El Grupo Teatro del 60 and El Nuevo Teatro Pobre de America, the latter created by playwright and director Pedro Santaliz. Santaliz trained and influenced a whole generation of theater people, including Jose (Papo) Marquez and Lydia Milagros Gonzalez, who became active in street theater in the 1970s, and Zora Moreno, who founded the community-based Teatro El Gran Quince in 1967 in the working-class Tokio barrio in San Juan.

NOTES

1. F. Arturo Rosales, "Spanish-Language Theatre and Early Mexican Immigration," in *Hispanic Theater in the United States,* ed. Nicolas Kanellos, Houston: Arte Publico Press, 1984, p. 20.

2. The beautiful colonial building still stands and is now being used by a local Black Elks chapter.

3. "Two Centuries of Hispanic Theatre in the Southwest," in *Mexican American Theatre: Then and Now,* ed. Nicolas Kanellos, Houston: Arte Publico Press, 1983, p. 35.

4. Tomas Ybarra-Frausto, "I Can Still Hear the Applause," in *Hispanic Theatre in the United States,* pp. 52-53.

5. *Ibid.,* p. 51.

6. *Tejanos, manitos,* and *californios* refer to Mexicans living in Texas, New Mexico, and California when those lands were still part of Mexico.

7. "I Can Still Hear the Applause," p. 54-55.

8. Pablo Figueroa, *Teatro: Hispanic Theatre in New York City: 1920-1976,* New York: El Museo del Barrio, 1977, p. 8.

9. Miriam Colon had come from Puerto Rico to New York in the 1950s to study at the Actors Studio. By the time she founded the Puerto Rican Traveling Theatre in 1967, she had appeared on Broadway, Off Broadway, in films and television. In 1972 she became a member of the New York State Council on the Arts, a position she held until 1985. Colon has played a major role in gaining recognition for Hispanic arts in the United States and has given untold encouragement to other New York-based Hispanic theater organizations.

10. *El Grito de Lares* refers to an 1868 uprising of the same name. Although the rebellion was quickly put down by the Spanish authorities, the date of that event became a semi-official holiday in Puerto Rico and is symbolic of the birth of Puerto Rican nationalism.

11. Gloria Feiman Waldman, "Luis Rafael Sanchez and the New Latin American Theatre" (Ph.D. dissertation, City University of New York, 1967), p. 478. My translation from Spanish.

3. Contemporary Hispanic Theater Movements: 1965-1985

INTRODUCTION

The political upheaval of the 1960s, sparked by the civil rights movement and the escalating Vietnam War, had a strong impact on the growth of contemporary Hispanic theater. Nowhere was this relationship clearer than in the emergence of El Teatro Campesino in 1965, which grew directly out of the ferment of the United Farmworkers' struggle in California. The 1960s also marked the re-emergence of Hispanic theater in New York, though the causes for its reappearance there were more complex, reflecting the greater diversity of New York's Hispanic population. In 1965 George Edgar and Stella Holt produced the English version of Puerto Rican playwright Rene Marques's *The Oxcart* Off Broadway, with Miriam Colon in the lead role; Roberto Rodriguez produced his play *Las Ventanas* at the Chelsea Theatre Center; Cuban refugee Gilberto Zaldivar produced the Spanish classic *La Celestina,* with fellow Cubans Andres Castro and Antonia Rey, at the Greenwich Mews Theatre; and the Real Great Society, a community-based organization with an arts component, was founded on New York's Lower East Side.

THE WEST

The growth of the Latino theater movement from Chicago westward during the last two decades was intimately tied to the work of El Teatro Campesino. Its founder Luis Valdez was a theater student at San Jose State College when Chavez's farmworkers' movement began to gain momentum. Born into a migrant farmworker family, Valdez had received theatrical training from the San Francisco Mime Troupe in the early 1960s. The influence of the Mime Troupe, as well as *carpa* teatro and Mexican vaudeville routines, were apparent in the early style of El Teatro Campesino.

Striking farmworkers from the vineyards of California were the first members of El Teatro Campesino. They created short theater pieces that dramatized their political struggle, their relations with the bosses, and their need for a strong union. Valdez called this new genre, which was "somewhere between Brecht and Cantinflas," an *acto*.[1] Humor and music, especially the Mexican *corrido,* became stock elements of the *acto* and remain central to Chicano theater today. Valdez used humor in his agit-prop work "because," he said, "it stems from a necessary situation—the necessity of lifting the morale of our strikers . . . This leads us into satire and the underlying tragedy of it all—the fact that human beings have been wasted in farm labor for generations."[2]

The *acto* had five objectives: the first was to inspire the audience to social action; second, to illuminate specific points about social problems; third, to satirize the opposition; fourth, to show or hint at a solution; and fifth, to express what people are thinking.[3] It could be put together quickly and required little theater training. The material grew out of improvisation that Valdez put into dramatic form. The troupe toured the grape region of central California and convinced farmworkers to join Chavez's union.

By 1969 the Farmworkers Union had gained strength and the original members of El Teatro Campesino had disbanded. Working with his students at Fresno State College, Valdez introduced elements of indigenous Mexican mythology into his work. He was criticized for abandoning the political struggle to concentrate on mythical and religious aspects of Chicano culture; in reality, however, those elements were not a departure but a return. Valdez had long been attracted to Mexican Indian cultures and had used such themes in his first two plays, *The Shrunken Head of Pancho Villa* and *Dark Root of a Scream,* written in 1964. Like many other artists from minority groups, Valdez combined his search for cultural identity with a commitment to address social issues. El Teatro Campesino had not lost its political fervor; rather, it had begun a process of experimentation and growth.

In the early 1970s almost one hundred Chicano theater groups, largely encouraged, inspired, and trained by El Teatro Campesino, flourished throughout the Southwest and the West. Most of the founders of these groups had no formal training, with the exception of Adrian Vargas, who started Teatro de la Gente in 1969, and Jorge Huerta, who founded El Teatro de la Esperanza the same year.

According to Yvonne Yarbro-Bejarano, this flowering of theatrical expression had deep roots in "the vast majority of Chicanos [having] . . . limited access to literacy and education. Chicano literary expression," she noted,

> has been largely popular in form and oral in transmission. . . the Chicano movement in the late sixties and early seventies . . . validate[d] popular and oral forms of cultural expression and . . . counter[ed] the lack of access to the mainstream literary establishment with the creation of a Chicano communications network . . . [including] community newspapers featuring the work of local, grass-roots poets. . . Chicano literary magazines and publishing houses.[4]

The Chicano theater groups that emerged were part of this effort.

Most teatros were community-based and represented a blending of the old and the new. *Actos* generally dramatized such community concerns as drug abuse, problems in the schools, and police brutality.[5] *Pastorelas,* or shepherds' plays, the traditional Nativity dramas dating to 16th-century Mexico when Spanish missionaries incorporated indigenous language, costumes, and dance into their religious plays, are still performed every year at Christmas time to enthusiastic audiences.

Dialogue reflected complex patterns of acculturation and resistance to the dominant Anglo culture. The language of Chicano theater was characterized by a mixture of English and Spanish, sometimes within one sentence. As Jorge Huerta described it,

> . . . the more recent arrivals from Mexico speak little or no English, while most Chicanos usually speak both Spanish and English to varying degrees. The majority of the plays produced for audiences will reflect this linguistic particularity, employing a mixture of Spanish and English as well as *calo,* the language of the streets . . . . Many Mexicans who do not speak English can understand it, and many Chicanos who do not communicate in Spanish can recognize the language of their parents . . . By addressing a bilingual public, teatros are asserting a very definite particularity that may arouse resentment among the non-bilingual members of the audience, especially the English-speakers. . . . however, most teatros speak to their specific communities, in their own languages.[6]

Valdez's concerns about artistic growth and development led him to organize the first Chicano theater festival. Held in Fresno in 1970, the festival showed the teatros new ways of approaching material and diverse styles from which to draw. Fifteen groups, including the Revelationists from New York, Pedro Santaliz's El Nuevo Teatro Pobre de America from Puerto Rico/New York, and Los Mascarones from Mexico, directed by Mariano Leyva, were invited. Leyva's charisma and his group's innovative work were very influential. Huerta attributed his impact to

> a very disciplined and effective form of choral poetry which had not been seen before in the teatro movement. Leyva's troupe was an important link with the Chicano's linguistic heritage, bringing the Spanish language to life for a people whose linguistic particularities had been a political drawback since the intrusion of the Anglo.[7]

Leyva was also instrumental in the formation in 1971 of TENAZ (Teatro Nacional de Aztlan), a coalition of Chicano theaters. TENAZ, which means "tenacious" in Spanish, continues to sponsor biannual theater festivals.

After the first festival, the teatros began to look to Latin America for ideas in style and dramaturgy. El Teatro Campesino created *La gran carpa de los Rascuachis,* its first collective full-length piece. El Teatro de la Esperanza adapted dramaturgical techniques of Colombian playwright Enrique Buenaventura and incorporated musical pieces from Chilean composer Luis Advis's cantata *The Siege of Santa Maria de Iquiqui,* which dramatized the massacre of 2,000 striking nitrate miners in the north of Chile in 1907. Teatro de la Gente adapted an Argentine play, using its dramaturgical technique of narration, a distinctly different style for them, but adding *corridos* to select scenes to keep the Mexican flavor.

During the 1970s, most teatros—including the ultra avant-garde Los Angeles-based group ASCO—were organized as collectives with no outside boards of directors; administrative and artistic decisions were made collectively.[8] The collective structure was a conscious political choice. It underscored the position that farmworkers and minorities should take a more active role in the political process and provided "the opportunity to work out in the daily practice of human relationships the ideology underlying the plays."[9] Jose Montoya, a pioneer of the teatro movement and co-founder in 1970 of Sacramento's Centro de Artistas Chicanos (also known as The Royal Chicano Air Force), asserted that the collective gave young people a home, a sense of belonging to something vital, and commitment to a common cause.

Today the era of the collective is all but over. Of the almost one hundred campesino-inspired teatros that sprang up throughout the West Coast, the Southwest, and the Midwest between 1965 and 1975, only five—El Teatro Campesino, El Teatro de la Esperanza, and El Teatro Urbano (now known as

Urbano Enterprises) in California; Su Teatro in Denver; and Teatro Libertad in Tucson—have survived. These groups are at different levels of artistic development and some are more active than others. All of them face organizational difficulties. Indeed, the collective structure and the difficulties inherent in sustaining the teatros may have contributed to the failure of many of them. Touring, which became their main source of income, demanded too much time away from home to develop local audiences, and also aggravated internal problems and burnout. Ironically, the very success of the Chicano movement, which produced access to mainstream employment, may also have accelerated the decline of many teatros.

In addition, the 1974 Chicano/Latin American Theatre Festival, held in Mexico City, set the Chicano theater movement back ten years, according to Valdez. Most U.S. teatros were quite new. They were concerned with ethnic identity and finding their cultural roots. Mexican and South American groups in attendance, who held strong leftist and Marxist points of view, chastised the Chicano groups for their lack of militancy. El Teatro Campesino was criticized for allowing religious images to appear in its work. That confrontation shook the self-confidence of the younger groups. Without *la causa* of Cesar Chavez's Farmworkers Union or a larger social movement to hold them together, it was difficult to regain that confidence. Many never did.

In 1976 two of the stronger groups rallied with pieces that have become milestones in the history of Chicano theater: El Teatro de la Esperanza introduced its most notable collective piece, *La Victima,* and El Teatro Campesino opened Luis Valdez's *Zoot Suit* at the Mark Taper Forum in Los Angeles. *La Victima* exhibited considerable stylistic growth as El Teatro de la Esperanza moved into a more complex form of semi-documentary theater. "Based on documented fact about the immigration and deportation of Mexicans, [*La Victima*] mingles history with fiction to create . . . a Mexican American who becomes an immigration officer and believes that he must [reject] his culture, his heritage and his identity to continue his chosen profession."[10] His alienation from his roots is objectified when he realizes that he has deported his own mother from whom he had been separated since childhood. Teatros all over the country have produced *La Victima,* and El Teatro de la Esperanza continues to tour the piece as one of the most popular of its repertory.

Zoot Suit caused a stir when it opened that is still not forgotten. "Valdez's play . . . [drew] on documentation and the playwright's imagination . . . [and] combined elements of the *acto, corrido, carpa,* and *mito* with Living Newspaper techniques to dramatize a Chicano family in crisis."[11] Based on the famous zoot suit riots of 1943 in Los Angeles, *Zoot Suit* dramatized the sensational Sleepy Lagoon trial of sixteen young Mexicans and Mexican Americans, focusing on the leader of the group and his love affair with the woman lawyer who led the defense committee. After the trial, brawls broke out between members of the *pachuco* gangs and off-duty U.S. servicemen. The flashy zoot suit, first introduced by blacks in the East, gave the young Mexican Americans who wore them an air of arrogance and alienation. What began as a few minor incidents quickly escalated into race riots: "an undeclared war on Mexican Americans by roving packs of undisciplined servicemen."[12] The Mexican Ambassador in Washington had to intervene with the U.S. State Department to bring the rioting under control. Two years later the convictions in the Sleepy Lagoon trial were overturned, but the victory could not offset the damage done to the image of the Mexican.

According to Jorge Huerta,

Zoot Suit . . . was supported by both Mechicanos and non-Hispanics who jumped to their feet at the close of each performance. Working class people sat next to season subscribers, each group experiencing distinct reactions . . . Valdez proved once and for all that the Chicano can produce a professional theater appealing to all people while not ignoring political realities.[13]

After its run at the Mark Taper Forum, *Zoot Suit* went on to enjoy a long commercial success in Los Angeles, a first for a Chicano play. It later opened on Broadway, another first, but did not fare as well in New York for reasons that had less to do with the play than with the choice of theater and methods of promotion.

Zoot Suit has had a major impact on other Chicano/Latino theaters, although Valdez was criticized for "commercializing" El Teatro Campesino at the time. The challenge of survival in the 1980s has also prompted change in Chicano theater. Theaters have become more concerned with artistry and their need for better administrative skills. Theaters that have sprung up in the past decade are more diverse in style, mission, and structure than the early teatros. At the TENAZ-sponsored 1984 Chicano/Latino Theatre Festival held in Santa Barbara, this pluralism was accepted as a sign of growth or, at least, as a fact of life in the 1980s.

THE EAST

New York

There is greater economic and cultural diversity among Hispanics on the East Coast, and this is reflected in Hispanic theater. When the mass migration of the Puerto Rican working people began in the 1940s, they settled almost exclusively in urban areas, but mostly in New York where they far outnumbered other Hispanic groups. Immigrants of varied economic backgrounds from the Dominican Republic, South America, and Cuba followed. Although they were ethnically diverse and lacked a unifying cause like the farmworkers' struggle, Hispanic artists in the East were also caught up in the unrest and social change of the 1960s. Some of the first public and private monies that became available to minority arts groups—in 1967—was in response to racial tensions and riots. The Real Great Society received city funds to support its Theatre of Courage, a training program for community youths, and Miriam Colon's Puerto Rican Traveling Theatre was able to take Hispanic plays in both English and Spanish to city parks during the summer.[14]

Many of the New York-based Puerto Rican theaters that emerged in the 1960s were grass-roots-oriented and community-based, like The Real Great Society on the Lower East Side and the Revelationists in East Harlem. Pedro Santaliz's Nuevo Pobre Teatro de America worked out of New York in those years, touching Puerto Rican youths all over the city. "Santaliz organized . . . workshops to provide the young Puerto Rican members [of his group] an awareness of the history and culture of their country, to allow them to rediscover—and sometimes discover for the first time—a national identity of which they could be proud, and to offer a training program for young Puerto Rican actors, directors and designers."[15] Santaliz is now based in San Juan.

The community theaters had an artistic vitality and integrity comparable to the teatros in the West. Caribbean bongos underscored lively plays and skits. Improvisation and circus techniques were used to develop theater pieces relevant to the lives of the people of the community. The Real Great Society—which changed its name to CHARAS, Inc. in 1970—is the only one of the groups with programs of community education and culture that is still functioning.

In 1966 I founded TOLA, Theatre of Latin America, Inc., after having lived for two and one-half years in Latin America working in the theater in Chile. TOLA was a pioneer in producing Latin American plays in English translation in New York; in the touring of Latin American theater companies, music groups, and theater people throughout the United States; and in the creation of networks between Latin American and U.S. theater people. TOLA received OBIE Awards for two of its productions, *Latin American Fair of Opinion* (1972) and *Chile! Chile!* (1976), and also built a valuable library of Latin American plays and reference books on Latin American theater.[16]

Cuban refugees began to produce plays in New York in the late 1960s. Some had theater backgrounds, others did not. Gilberto Zaldivar and Rene Buch, who founded Repertorio Español in 1968, were theatrically trained.[17] Zaldivar's productions of *La Celestina* at the Greenwich Mews and *Yerma* at Theater East convinced him that there was an audience in New York for Spanish-language plays. He and Rene Buch opened Repertorio Español's first production, the Spanish classic *La Dama Duende*, at the Greenwich Mews in 1968. They moved to their East 27th Street theater in 1972. INTAR (International Arts Relations), on the other hand, was founded by seven young Cubans and Puerto Ricans with little or no theater experience. In 1966 they rented a loft under the name ADAL with monies from fund-raising events. Among the first plays ADAL produced were Spanish translations of Ionesco's *La Cantatrice Chauve* and a Brazilian play, *As Maños de Euridice*. They had hoped to run their theater on a commercial basis, but, on Miriam Colon's advice, they became incorporated as a not-for-profit organization in 1972 under the name INTAR.[18]

In 1969 Magali Alabau and Manuel Martin opened Teatro Duo, a tiny 27-seat theater on East 12th Street. Its name bespoke its dual role: to produce contemporary Latin American and U.S. plays in English and Spanish. Martin had come to the United States from Cuba in the early 1950s with no theatrical background; but Alabau, who arrived in 1967, had been trained in theater in Cuba. With Alabau's encouragement, Martin became a director and playwright. Duo produced its first play, *Penitents* by Roberto Rodriguez, in 1969. The play dramatized the desire for Puerto Rican independence from the United States by focusing on the draft and the loss of Puerto Rican lives in Vietnam. It also produced a Spanish-language version of Leonard Melfi's *Birdbath*, called *La*

Palangana. In the 1970s Teatro Duo had brief residencies at INTAR and at La Mama Experimental Theater Club. (La Mama has been hospitable to U.S. Hispanic and Latin American companies since the mid-1960s.) Duo now has a permanent home on East 4th Street, a few buildings away from La Mama.

The first Cuban-run theaters in New York presented conventional European plays in Spanish and translations of European classics and contemporary U.S. plays. The Puerto Rican community theaters, however, integrated various theater and performance genres to create new styles. Their writers often wrote in the language of the streets of the city, an anglicized Spanish called "Spanglish."

New community-oriented theater organizations appeared in the early 1970s. The Nuyorican Poets Cafe, now located on East 3rd Street, was established by Miguel Algarin to give Puerto Rican artists a showcase and to serve the community of the Lower East Side. Playwrights Miguel Piñero and Lucky Cienfuegos and poets Algarin and Sandra Esteves have worked out of the Poets Cafe. The Family Repertory Company was created in 1972, when ex-prisoners who had participated in Marvin Felix Camillo's theater workshops at the Bedford Correctional Facility in Westchester County wanted to continue their involvement with theater and approached Camillo with the idea of starting a permanent group. Most of its early members were either Hispanic or black. Camillo, himself of Mexican and black heritage, directed the group's first piece, Miguel Piñero's *Short Eyes,* which brilliantly recreated the microsociety of prison life. Camillo's staging received an OBIE award in 1973. Pedro Pietri's Latin Insomniacs collective, founded in 1973, has nurtured the work of Puerto Rican playwrights, poets, and directors. It has never actively sought outside funding, preferring to maintain its loosely structured organization of artists who support one another's work.

1975 to 1985 were years of artistic and managerial growth for the Hispanic theaters in New York that survived. INTAR, Puerto Rican Traveling Theatre, and Repertorio Español, which now have annual budgets in excess of $500,000, are the most notable. Some dozen new theater organizations were established, among them the Association of Hispanic Arts (AHA). Marta Moreno Vega, a strong advocate for the promotion and recognition of Hispanic arts in New York, founded AHA in 1975 to strengthen ties among New York Hispanic arts organizations and to create a united base for stronger Hispanic arts advocacy.

The growth of the Puerto Rican Traveling Theatre, Repertorio Español, and INTAR began in the late 1970s, when they focused their artistic missions and/or moved into permanent theater spaces. Repertorio Español concentrated on Spanish classics, which have become its forte. Its repertory also includes contemporary Latin American and U.S. Hispanic plays, Spanish *zarzuelas,* and music and dance programs, all performed in Spanish. The company has developed a touring circuit reaching as far west as San Antonio and Tucson. INTAR's decision to move to 42nd Street's Theatre Row in 1978 and to produce only in English forced organizational maturity. The decision to present English-language productions of Hispanic plays was heavily criticized at first by the Hispanic community, but INTAR argued that as the only Hispanic theater on Theatre Row the change would attract a wider audience and increase its visibility. It also provided opportunities for new Hispanic playwrights who write in English. Developing and staging new material has become INTAR's primary contribution to Hispanic theater.[19]

In 1979 the Puerto Rican Traveling Theatre moved to its present location on West 47th Street in the Broadway area. Colon raised close to $3 million to renovate an old firehouse into a well-equipped 196-seat theater and rehearsal space. The organization produces contemporary Latin American and Spanish plays, along with Puerto Rican and U.S. Hispanic plays, in both English and Spanish. It has also maintained its summer touring program in New York City parks.

Thalia Spanish Theatre made artistic and managerial changes when Silvio Brito took over its direction in 1978. Thalia was founded in 1969 as the Dume Theater and run by Cuban exile Herberto Dume until he moved to Miami. Brito moved the theater to Queens, changed its name, and made the decision to produce plays only from Spain in Spanish. Its institutional growth has not been as dramatic as the theaters mentioned above, but it produces ongoing seasons of plays and is addressing new audiences.

CHARAS, Inc. and the Nuyorican Poets Cafe have been strengthened institutionally by renovating permanent spaces for their programs with substantial capital funding grants from the city. The Nuyorican Poets Cafe is renovating a small five-story building on East 3rd Street to house its cafe and offices. CHARAS is renovating an abandoned public school in the same neighborhood; it took over the school in 1978 under the city's Adopt-a-Building program.

CHARAS has become a lively community cultural center, offering programming in performing and visual arts, and film, as well as such community services as adult education and day care. Both organizations run their artistic seasons on relatively small budgets.

New theaters that have appeared during the past decade cover a wide range of activity and artistic quality. At least six are located outside Manhattan—in the Bronx, Queens, and Brooklyn. Only one is budgeted over $80,000. Most theater groups in New York are now more concerned about achieving organizational stability than they were ten to fifteen years ago, but some groups and artists will always prefer to do their work without the constraints of institutionalization.

Miami

Miami has been a difficult city in which to establish serious Hispanic theater (although there has been significant progress in the past few years). The first wave of Cuban refugees who settled in Miami immediately after the 1959 revolution had been exposed at home mainly to vaudeville theater and comedy revues. Those genres dominate most Cuban-run theaters in Miami.[20]

Audience predilections coupled with Cuban distrust for government arts funding presented serious handicaps to the development of Hispanic theater in Miami. Cuban producers were completely isolated from the world of minority arts funding. Everything—whether vaudeville, low comedy, political satire, or serious plays—was done in Spanish; and serious plays were almost always translations of U.S. or European plays. Cuban writers who remained in Miami continued to write in Spanish; those who write in English do not live in Miami.

The serious theater that exists in Miami today comes from a variety of sources. Teresa Maria Rojas, who came in 1962, had received dramatic training in Havana. In 1972 she founded the Teatro Prometeo at Miami-Dade Community College, which allowed her to take more risks in style and content than she could have in commercial theater. The following year, Mario Ernesto Sanchez founded the Avante Theatre. Sanchez's repertory includes Latin American and Cuban plays and Spanish translations of more conventional U.S. and European works. In 1980 the Mariel boatlift brought several young theater people to Miami who injected new ideas into the theater community. Jose Ferrer's brief but important tenure as artistic director of the Coconut Grove Playhouse, from 1983 to 1985 brought a new respectability to the playhouse and introduced a Hispanic program that his successors are maintaining. Finally, to encourage and strengthen Hispanic theater in Miami, Acting Together, a coalition of Miami-based Cuban theaters, was formed in 1984 through the initiative of Olga Garay-Ahern of the Metro-Dade Cultural Affairs Council.

PUERTO RICO

Puerto Rico's cultural history has not followed the course of U.S. Hispanic theater movements, but rather European, U.S., and Latin American artistic trends. Its theater expressions cover a broad range, from conventional to the avant-garde, from highly commercialized to community-based productions. Most theaters in Puerto Rico, though incorporated as not-for-profit organizations, lack strong administrative staffs, have not applied for tax-exempt status, and receive little non-earned money from government or private sources.

Four theater organizations formed in the 1960s remain active: Producciones Cisne, El Grupo Teatro del 60, El Nuevo Teatro Pobre de America, and Teatro El Gran Quince. Producciones Cisne presents solid productions, usually of conventional plays. El Grupo Teatro del 60 emphasizes Puerto Rican themes and more contemporary forms. Pedro Santaliz, who formed the Nuevo Teatro Pobre de America in 1964, spent the mid-1960s in New York training young Puerto Ricans in theater techniques. Influenced in part by Santaliz, Zora Moreno in 1967 founded Teatro El Gran Quince in the Tokio barrio, a working-class neighborhood in the heart of San Juan.[21] Ramon A. (Moncho) Conde, its current director, creates theater pieces based on the interests of communities throughout the island for whom the group performs. In 1978 Moreno founded another theater, Producciones Flor de Cahillo. She produces her own plays and is gaining a reputation as a writer. Another young woman, Teresa Marichal, has recently emerged as a playwright of interest. She writes on women's themes; her style is nonrealistic, bordering on the abstract.

Gilda Navarra's dance theater, Taller de Histriones, Juan Gonzalez's Producciones Candilejas, and Carlos Ferrari's Nuestro Teatro were established in the 1970s. Navarra was trained as a flamenco dancer, then studied mime in Paris.

She has used her skills to train hundreds of students over the years and has created many original dance theater pieces that toured the island annually until 1985 when the company was dissolved. Ferrari produces his own nontraditional, socially conscious plays in Nuestro Teatro's permanent theater space. Gonzalez, who has a reputation as San Juan's shrewdest commercial producer, has built a production company that books limited runs of national and international plays for performance in rented spaces, usually the 700-seat Tapia Theatre in Old San Juan.

In 1981 the Centro de Bellas Artes, built and supported by the government, opened in San Juan. It houses three theater spaces, which are booked by local and international companies.

THE ROLE OF WOMEN IN U.S. HISPANIC THEATER

Chicano women have had a more difficult struggle for recognition in theater than Hispanic women in New York, Miami, or Puerto Rico. The collective structure of the early teatros was a mixed blessing for Chicanas. It gave them the opportunity of actively participating in the decision-making process, yet they were expected to take care of the children during rehearsals and to stay home with them while their companies went on tour. Silviana Wood, a playwright from Tucson, Arizona, and a member of Teatro Libertad until 1980 when she formed her own group, used to solve the problem by writing children's roles into her plays so her children could be with her.

When a women's teatro, Teatro Raices, was formed in San Diego in 1971, its members were accused of being lesbians by men and whores by other women in the teatro movement. The men felt that Teatro Raices' material exaggerated their *machismo*; the women charged that the Teatro Raices women wanted their men. Members of Teatro Raices felt their work was too harshly criticized as unprofessional and artistically undeveloped. Felicitas Nuñez and Delia Revelo, two founders of the group, wanted to use the teatro to dramatize changes in women's lives. They adapted to a southern California setting Brecht's *The Mother* and *The Salt of the Earth*, a movie about striking Southwestern mineworkers whose women picketed in their place. The group was active on a part-time basis until 1982.

Women In Teatro (WIT), founded in California in 1978, represented a different kind of effort on behalf of Hispanic women in theater. It aimed at stimulating all aspects of women's artistic growth by identifying problems that specifically relate to *mujeres* in teatro, forming a support group, and establishing a communication network. In 1980 WIT outlined several objectives: the need for women playwrights, producers, and directors; strong women's roles; community support for the development of women in teatro; and child care.[22]

WIT was instrumental in gaining recognition for Chicanas and developing their leadership ability. A woman now sits on the TENAZ coordinating council; TENAZ sponsored the first Women's Seminario at its festival in Santa Barbara in 1979; and El Teatro de la Esperanza hosted the festival's first women's teatro workshop. TENAZ also adopted a child-care policy and is sensitive to gender representation on its board of directors and on festival critique panels. Workshops now support women's professional growth at festivals; and plays that educate the public on positive male and female roles are encouraged. Carolina Flores, one of WIT's founders and a strong advocate for women in theater, believes that "it is the responsibility of women working in theater to introduce new images of women to the stage which will, in turn, establish new images for men."[23] In 1984, Flores co-founded Teatro Huipil, now called Teatro Vision, a women's theater group in San Jose, California.

Cuban and Puerto Rican women have played prominent roles in theater on the East Coast and in Puerto Rico. Today's generation of Puerto Rican women playwrights can find role models as far back as the 19th century. Victoria Espinoza, one of Puerto Rico's most talented and respected directors, now heads the theater program at the Instituto de Cultura Puertorriqueña. Senator Velda Gonzalez, herself an actress with a children's theater group, has key influence over government appropriations for the arts.

In New York, the names Marta Moreno Vega and Miriam Colon are synonymous with leadership in Hispanic arts. Vega has been instrumental in bringing New York State and New York City legislative attention to Hispanic Arts, and Miriam Colon has worked at both the state and national levels to promote and defend the rights of Hispanic artists. Both women founded and direct their own arts organizations: Colon, the Puerto Rican Traveling Theatre; and Vega, the Caribbean Cultural Center.

In Miami, Cuban-American Olga Garay-Ahern, now assistant director of the

Metro-Dade Cultural Affairs Council, plays a major role in efforts to strengthen Miami-based Hispanic theaters. Other Hispanic women who have made important contributions to Hispanic theaters in New York include Magali Alabau, Silvia Brito, Lourdes Casals, Alba Olms, Elsa Ortiz, Ilka Tanya Payan, and Margarita Toraic. In addition, Hispanic theater in the United States boasts a substantial number of women playwrights, including Lynn Alvarez, Maria Irene Fornes, Dolores Prida, and Ana Maria Simo in New York; Milcha Sanchez Scott and Edit Villarreal in Los Angeles; Denise Chavez in Las Cruces, New Mexico; Estela Portillo Tramblay in El Paso, Texas; and Silviana Wood in Tucson, Arizona. Their plays cover a wide range of styles and themes. Unfortunately, there is little communication among them. One of the goals of WIT had been to build a network of women playwrights, starting with those who were TENAZ members. A meeting of women writers planned by TENAZ in the early 1980s never materialized.

NOTES

1. Jorge A. Huerta, *Chicano Theatre: Themes and Forms,* Ypsilanti, Michigan: Bilingual Press/Editorial Bilingúe, 1982, p. 18.

2. *Ibid.,* p. 18.

3. *Ibid.,* p. 16.

4. "Chicanas' Experience in Collective Theatre: Ideology and Form," Unpublished manuscript, p. 2.

5. Jorge A. Huerta, "Labor Theatre, Street Theatre and Community Theatre in the Barrios, 1965-1983," in *Hispanic Theater in the United States,* ed. Nicolas Kanellos, Houston: Arte Publico Press, 1984, p. 65.

6. *Chicano Theatre,* p. 6.

7. "The Influence of Latin American Theatre on Teatro Chicano," in *Mexican American Theatre: Then and Now,* ed. Nicolas Kanellos, Houston, Arte Publico Press, 1983, p. 70.

8. Only the Bilingual Foundation of the Arts (BFA), founded in Los Angeles in 1973 by Carmen Zapata, Margarita Galban, and Estela Scarlata was patterned after U.S. and New York Cuban-run not-for-profit theater organizations, with an outside board of directors and an ongoing season of plays. Zapata, a New Yorker of Mexican and Argentine background; Galban, a middle-class Cuban; and Scarlata, an Argentine; had years of professional theater experience behind them, all European-U.S. in style.

9. Yarbro-Bejarano, "Chicanas' Experience in Collective Theatre," p. 3.

10. Huerta, *Chicano Theatre,* p. 49.

11. *Ibid.,* p. 177.

12. Meier and Rivera, *The Chicanos,* New York: Hill & Wang, 1972, p. 193.

13. *Chicano Theatre,* p. 219.

14. Some of the community-based groups did not have the necessary administrative skills to take advantage of the funding; others did not want to accept the money for political reasons. The latter was also true on the West Coast. El Teatro Campesino, for example, did not accept a grant from the National Endowment for the Arts until 1975, and was then highly criticized by fellow teatros for having "sold out." Campesino's first grant from the NEA program geared to minority arts groups (Expansion Arts, created in 1971) was in 1979.

15. Joanne Pottlitzer, "Viva la Revelation!," *Theatre 2*, ed. by International Theatre Institute: New York, 1970, p. 130.

16. The TOLA library collection is now housed at the U.S. Centre of the International Theatre Institute in New York City.

17. Buch came to this country in 1948 to study theater at Yale and never returned to Cuba. When Zaldivar arrived in New York in 1961, he worked as a lighting technician at the Cricket Theatre and later as business manager at the Greenwich Mews Theatre for Stella Holt and Frances Drucker, who trained him in Off Broadway theater production. He was business manager of the Puerto Rican Traveling Theatre's summer parks program from 1968 to 1971.

18. Max Ferra, INTAR's artistic director, is the only original member of ADAL who has remained consistently with the organization.

19. In 1981 a four-year grant of $150,000 from the Ford Foundation helped launch INTAR's annual Hispanic Playwrights-in-Residence Laboratory conducted by Maria Irene Fornes. In 1985 INTAR initiated a music theater laboratory to encourage Hispanic artists to create musicals.

20. A major theater owner, Ernesto Capote, who had been a set and lighting designer for the Tropicana nightclub in Havana, catered to the demand for vaudeville and added a showtime flavor when he opened his first theater in Miami in 1969. His seven theaters and three movie houses, which operate year round are feeling the effect of cable television and videocassette recorders. Salvador Ugarte and Alfonso Cremata, who own two small, but financially successful theaters called "Las Mascaras," had been unsuccessful when they staged translations of American and European plays in the late 1960s; so they turned to original comedy farces with sexual puns and slapstick.

21. Zora Moreno was born and raised in Tokio. She became interested in theater when she played the role of the Virgin Mary each year in the barrio's passion play. Her local priest helped finance her early theatrical training.

22. El Teatro de la Esperanza was the first teatro to establish a child-care policy.

23. Conversation with Flores, 1986.

4. Current Hispanic Theater Activity

INTRODUCTION

What is a Hispanic play? Is it one written in Spanish? Is it one with Hispanic content? What about Hispanic playwrights who write in English and whose material is not tied to a Hispanic issue or theme? "If you're in Bolivia writing in Spanish and you make a play as abstract as Ionesco, you're still a Latin American playwright. In this country, writing in English, it's an identity crisis," says New York-Cuban playwright Ana Maria Simo.[1] Veteran playwright Maria Irene Fornes comments, "In a Hispanic play, the point of view, how people feel, the way they treat each other, are not American. We all have Iberian ancestry, speak Spanish; we're all Catholic. A Hispanic playwright, one with Hispanic upbringing, will have a different temperament from an American, different recollections, different enemies. . . . And don't harass me by asking if a Chicano has the same temper as a Cuban; he doesn't. But still. Either you assume a Hispanic sensibility exists or it doesn't."[2]

Chicano theaters today do not have the single style or artistic vision they had ten or fifteen years ago. Puerto Rican and Cuban theaters in New York are not homogeneous. Even Cuban theater in Miami is beginning to diversify. The national survey of 145 Hispanic theater organizations reported on in this paper was conducted between April 1984 and April 1985, a time when many theaters were reevaluating their artistic direction and organizational growth. The survey was updated, when possible, in 1987.

The year of the survey was also a period of heightened controversy over American immigration policy, increased assimilation, and continued growth of the Hispanic population in the United States. In 1985 the *New York Times* pointed out that "The United States is now the seventh largest Spanish-speaking country."[3] It went on to note that between 1 million and 1.5 million Central Americans now live in the United States, some illegally. Media coverage of such issues as illegal aliens and bilingual education has made the general public more aware of Hispanics' presence, though in some cases it has aroused fears that Hispanics will remain an unassimilable mass. Several articles in *U.S. News and World Report* drew attention to the rapid growth of Hispanics in the United States and their potential influence on national politics, but noted that because of low voting rates Hispanics are generally not yet well-represented on the state and local levels.[5]

Despite high rates of unemployment and school dropout, Hispanics are finding more mainstream employment, including jobs in the arts. Edward James Olmos, who acted with El Teatro Campesino and other teatros, has won an Emmy and a Golden Globe Award for his role on the television series *Miami Vice*. Chicano actors are finding more work with mainstream theaters on the West Coast, and the works of New York-based Cuban playwright Eduardo Machado are produced by mainstream theaters throughout the country. Panamanian Ruben Blades was the first salsa/pop artist to appear on a mainstream label. His album *Searching for America* was a hit with Hispanics and non-Hispanics alike.

Hispanic arts leaders are concerned about the dangers of assimilation or "crossover." Speaking about his successful film *Crossover Dreams*, Blades says, "I find the whole idea of crossover dangerous, because it implies the abandonment of one base for another. I'd rather talk about convergence—the idea of two sides meeting in the middle of the bridge."[6] Luis Valdez also favors convergence; but Jose Montoya, co-founder of the Centro de Artistas Chicanos in Sacramento, believes that more education and jobs for Mexican Americans have resulted in a weakened sense of community. He fears that the growing Chicano middle class, including theater people, is losing its cultural identity. Jorge Huerta warns Chicano teatros that cultural and political apathy can be biproducts of success and stability.

Certain cultural changes will be inevitable for Hispanics, as they have been for minorities who preceded them in the United States. Many trained Hispanic actors already have a lessened sense of ethnicity. But Hispanic culture is also influencing mainstream America's music, food, dance, language, and the arts, especially literature.

Valdez is not troubled by his dual cultural identity; he thinks of himself as an American whose people have been Americans for hundreds of years before him. "I am writing new American theater,"[7] he says, and he fully expects his work to influence the temper of American theater generally.

As the following section illustrates, when we move beyond controversies over definitions of Hispanic theater, cultural assimilation, and American immigration policy, we see that Valdez's optimism about dual cultural identity is reflected in a healthy proliferation of Hispanic theater activity throughout the nation.

THE UNITED STATES HISPANIC THEATER SURVEY: NATIONAL DATA

The 145 Hispanic theater organizations surveyed included 101 theater groups, 28 presenting organizations, and 16 service organizations. The survey does not include every Hispanic theater organization in the United States, but it does provide an overview of Hispanic theater today along with specific information on the organizations surveyed.[8]

Of the 101 theater groups surveyed, 29 are run by Chicanos; 24 by Cubans; 11 by Puerto Ricans living on the U.S. mainland, 9 of whom are in New York City; 17 by San Juan-based Puerto Ricans; and 20 by Hispanics of other national backgrounds, non-Hispanics, or people of mixed cultural heritage.

Thirty-four theater organizations are in New York City. There are thirty-one organizations in California, eleven of which are in Los Angeles; and thirty-two in the Southwest, sixteen of which are in Texas. Florida has eighteen organizations, with seventeen in Miami and one in Tampa. The Midwest has the fewest theaters—four in Chicago and one in Minneapolis. The survey includes twenty-one theater organizations in San Juan, Puerto Rico.

Data collected from 87 of the 101 theater groups show that 30 of the 87 groups were founded since 1980 and that seven are twenty years old or more. Most theaters produce an average of three plays a year in 100- to 199-seat houses. Only 13 are affiliated with Actors Equity Association. Although nearly 50 percent of the theaters do not have paid staff, 85 percent pay their actors. Four of the 87 have annual budgets over $500,000; 20 are budgeted between $100,000 and $499,999; 28 between $20,000 and $99,000; 32 have budgets under $20,000. (Three had no budgets at the time of the survey.) Fifty-one groups receive state and local funding and money from private philanthropies; 34 receive funding from the National Endowment for the Arts; all groups earn some revenue.

The survey shows that the plays produced by these theater groups vary widely, depending on their particular mission and the language of their intended audience. Most Mexican American/Chicano theaters perform original collective works, plays by Chicano authors or adaptations of Latin American, U.S., or European plays. They usually perform bilingually, using both English and Spanish words, a reflection of the way they speak. New York Puerto Rican theaters perform original works in English or in their particular version of "Spanglish." All Cuban theaters in Miami and most Cuban theaters in New York perform only in Spanish. New York-based Cuban and Puerto Rican playwrights along with Latin American and Spanish authors are produced in New York. Miami theaters produce original low-comedy plays, Spanish translations of U.S. and European plays, and occasionally a Cuban or Latin American play. The Bilingual Foundation of the Arts in Los Angeles, Teatro Duo, Puerto Rican Traveling Theatre in New York and Borderlands Theatre/Teatro Fronterizo in Tucson are among the few theaters dedicated to presenting plays in both Spanish and English.

EAST COAST (New York, Connecticut, District of Columbia, Florida)

Fifty-five theater organizations, including forty-three theater groups, seven presenting organizations, and five service organizations, were surveyed on the East Coast.

New York
New York City: 25 theater groups, 6 presenting organizations, 3 service organizations*

New York City's Hispanic population is the largest and most diverse in the country. It is also the poorest. Of the more than 2 million Hispanics who live in New York, over 1 million are Puerto Rican, a figure larger than the population of San Juan. Almost 600,000 Dominicans and some 300,000 to 400,000 Colombians live in the city. Cubans and Central and other South Americans make up the rest of the Hispanic population. Most middle-class Cubans and South Americans live in Queens, but the great majority of Hispanics live in deprived areas of Manhattan and the South Bronx.

---

*Since the 1984-1985 survey was conducted, two theater groups have closed, and two new theater groups have been established in New York City. Hispanic Organization of Latin Actors (HOLA) is considered a producing organization in the statistical data.

The ethnic distribution of New York's Hispanic theaters does not correspond to the breakdown of the city's Hispanic population. Of the thirty-one theater groups and presenters surveyed, thirteen are run by Cubans, nine are Puerto Rican, six are Latin American, and three are multi-ethnic. Eight of the nine Puerto Rican groups are community-based and present their work in English. The Puerto Rican Traveling Theatre, which is not community-based but located in the theater district on West 47th Street, produces both in English and Spanish. Nine Cuban-run theater groups produce only in Spanish. Of the remaining four, INTAR and two children's theaters produce only in English; Teatro Duo works in both languages.[9] The six Latin American-run groups present work in English and Spanish; the multi-ethnic groups produce in English.

Five theater groups operate outside Manhattan: Thalia Spanish Theatre and Ollantay Center for the Arts in Queens; the Typical Theatre of Brooklyn; and the African Caribbean Poetry Theatre and Pregones Touring Puerto Rican Collective in the Bronx.[10]

Queens. Thalia and Ollantay, both run by Cubans, are addressing the Central and South American population in Queens. Both organizations began working in that borough in the late 1970s and present plays in Spanish. Thalia, which has its own theater in the Sunnyside section of Queens, presents plays and *zarzuelas* from Spain alone in order to avoid favoring any Latin American country. Ollantay, located in Jackson Heights, presents plays from Latin America and the Caribbean in its permanent storefront gallery space, then takes them "on tour" to Latin American cultural and community centers throughout the borough of Queens.

The Bronx. The African Caribbean Poetry Theatre was founded in 1980 by poet Sandra Esteves and playwright Juan Shamsu Alam to present programs of Puerto Rican music, poetry, and theater to the communities of the Bronx and greater New York City. The Poetry Theatre develops and produces new plays, among them works by Alam, whose plays have also been produced by INTAR, The Family Repertory Company, and South Street Theatre. Because the organization has no permanent space, it produces at various venues in the Bronx, including the Lehman Center for the Performing Arts and the Invisible Performance Workshop.

Manhattan. Six producing theater organizations in New York have relatively high profiles: Amistad World Theatre, INTAR, Puerto Rican Traveling Theatre,

Repertorio Español, Teatro Duo, and Thalia Spanish Theatre. All but Thalia are located in Manhattan. All but Repertorio Español and Thalia, which perform only in Spanish, produce under Equity contracts. INTAR, Puerto Rican Traveling Theatre, and Repertorio Español are the most established of the six, with annual budgets in excess of $500,000; Thalia's budget is slightly over $100,000; Duo and Amistad, under $50,000. INTAR, in addition to its play-production program, operates an art gallery that exhibits year-round. It also sponsors a playwrights lab conducted by Maria Irene Fornes and a music theater lab to encourage Hispanics to write and compose for musical theater. INTAR's labs, like its productions, are in English. INTAR's most important contributions to Hispanic theater are its playwrights' and composers' labs and its policy of producing at least one new play a season developed in the labs.

Repertorio Español found its niche within New York Hispanic theater by producing Spanish classics in the original. Although the classics remain the forte of its repertory, it also produces contemporary plays from Spain, Latin America, and the United States; Spanish *zarzuelas*; and music and dance programs. In addition to a full repertory season in its 140-seat house on East 27th Street, Repertorio Español now presents music-theater productions three to four times a month at the Equitable Center's 487-seat theater on 51st Street and 7th Avenue.

The Puerto Rican Traveling Theatre is the only New York Puerto Rican theater that is not community-based. It produces a season of Latin American, Puerto Rican, and U.S. Hispanic plays and maintains a summer program touring city parks throughout the five boroughs.

Teatro Duo produces contemporary Hispanic and non-Hispanic U.S. plays, sometimes in English, sometimes in Spanish, at its 99-seat theater on East 4th Street. It commissions and develops new plays by U.S. Hispanic writers, among them works by one of its artistic directors, Manuel Martin.

Amistad World Theatre is a multi-ethnic theater founded by Samuel Barton in 1981 to produce new plays. It practices nontraditional casting and often works out of INTAR 2 on West 53rd Street. Amistad has a workshop program to develop new Hispanic plays.

In addition to these established theater groups, Manhattan has a wide variety of art centers, workshops, presenting organizations, and advocacy groups. The

Arts for Living Center at the Henry Street Settlement is the largest arts center on the Lower East Side. The center is designed to serve the black, Jewish, and Hispanic residents of the area, but its emphasis has been largely black. Ed Figueroa, who is also associated with the New Rican Village in Spanish Harlem, conducts the New Federal Theatre's Latino Workshop as part of Woody King's multi-ethnic theater program at the Henry Street Settlement. Figueroa teaches the workshop twice a week, using new material that may result in a full production. The Latino Playwrights Reading Workshop Series, run by Puerto Rican-Cuban actress Carla Pinza to develop Hispanic writers for theater, television, and film, operated out of Henry Street for eleven years until 1986. It now holds its workshops at Goddard Community Cultural Center on Columbus Avenue and presents readings at different venues in Manhattan.

CHARAS, Inc. and the Nuyorican Poets Cafe are smaller arts centers on the Lower East Side. CHARAS is a grass-roots community center with youth, child-care, and community development programs, in addition to programs in theater, film, music, and visual arts. Carlos (Chino) Garcia, the center's director, was one of its founders. Its theater program is run by Bimbo Rivas, who acted in the original production of Miguel Piñero's *Short Eyes*. Rivas also acts with the Talking Band, a New York theater group directed by Paul Zimet. The plays at CHARAS are developed out of improvisational workshops with neighborhood people.

The Nuyorican Poets Cafe offers a forum for poets, playwrights, and musicians to perform their work. Its audiences come from all over the city. Closed for major renovations to its East 3rd Street building, the cafe reopened in the fall of 1987. Its performance and rehearsal spaces and offices now occupy the entire five-floor building.

Another theater organization of note operating on the Lower East Side is The Family Repertory Company, directed by its founder Marvin Felix Camillo. The family is a multi-ethnic theater organization that produces original works and adaptations of the classics. In addition to its productions, the company conducts acting and voice workshops and hosts Saturday night cabarets to encourage new talent. It also runs a community outreach program and brings its theater workshops to prisons throughout New York State and New Jersey.[11]

Rincon Taino, a younger organization, also operates on the Lower East Side, on Suffolk Street. Founded in 1983, Taino presents Latin American plays, music, and visual arts. The performing space and gallery are run by a Uruguayan, an Ecuadorian, a Dominican, and a Puerto Rican. Its resident theater LATEA, as well as invited groups and artists, reflect that cultural diversity.

The Americas Society and Taller Latinoamericano both house arts centers in Manhattan. The Americas Society's theater program, run by Argentine Alberto Minero, presents staged readings of U.S. Hispanic and Latin American plays. It also hosts receptions for and lectures and performances by visiting Latin American theater artists at its Park Avenue residence to introduce Latin American theater to the center's membership and the general public. Taller Latinamericano, located on East 2nd Street, is an arts and education center where performing artists, especially music groups and musicians, from all over the world can try out their work. The Taller runs an accredited language school.

The summer Festival Latino in New York, produced annually at the New York Shakespeare Festival's Public Theatre, is the largest presenter in the country of Latin American and U.S. Hispanic theater, music, and dance.[12] Argentine Oscar Ciccone and Salvadoran Cecilia Vega have managed the Festival Latino since 1974. It became an annual event in 1983, and in 1985 it received the official sponsorship of the Shakespeare Festival. The following year, the festival had grown from a seven- to ten-day run into an ambitious three-week event with performances at the Public Theatre, the Delacorte Theatre, and in hotels in New York State's Catskill Mountains.

The Association of Hispanic Arts (AHA), founded in 1975 to establish ties among Hispanic arts organizations in New York and to act as an advocate for strengthening Hispanic arts in New York City, now has a $300,000 budget. Under the directorship of Jane Delgado, AHA publishes a monthly newsletter on current Hispanic arts events and funding information, holds seminars and workshops on funding techniques, and provides promotional assistance for performing and visual arts events.

The Hispanic Organization of Latin Actors (HOLA), also established in 1975, serves the Hispanic theater community by publishing a monthly newsletter and a bi-annual directory of working Hispanic actors. HOLA, directed by Panamanian

Carlos Carrasco, an actor himself, also produces an annual festival of Latin American and U.S. Hispanic plays.

Of the twenty-four New York theater organizations included in the statistical figures at the end of this report, three have budgets in excess of $500,000; four are budgeted between $100,000 and $499,999; two between $50,000 and $99,999; nine have budgets between $25,000 and $49,999; and six are budgeted under $10,000.

Connecticut
New Haven: 1 theater group

The United Theatre of the Americas/Teatro Unido de las Americas, established in 1978, is a low-budget organization that produces bilingual productions of Latin American, Spanish, Puerto Rican, and U.S. Hispanic plays. It serves a constituency of some 16,000 Hispanics in New Haven and 150,000 throughout the state of Connecticut, most of whom are South American or Puerto Rican.

District of Columbia
Washington, D.C.: 2 theater groups

Since 1979, the Hispanic population of Washington, D.C. has more than doubled because of the influx of Salvadoran refugees. It is estimated that there are now over 250,000 Hispanics living in the metropolitan area, of which some 70 percent are from Central America. South Americans make up the second largest Hispanic group in Washington.

Grupo de Artistas Latinoamericanas (GALA) and Teatro Nuestro, founded in 1976 and 1978 respectively, have annual budgets between $60,000 and $80,000. Their performances attract both non-Hispanics and Hispanics. GALA, directed by Argentine Hugo Medrano, produces Latin American plays and original pieces in Spanish or English. Its theater space is part of a cultural complex for minority performing arts groups in downtown Washington. Teatro Nuestro, a community-based and community-oriented theater located near Columbia Road, performs in Hispanic neighborhoods throughout Washington D.C. Its theater pieces evolve out of improvisational workshops. For the past several years, it has focused on Central America since half its members emigrated from there. Performances are in English.

Florida: 15 theater groups, 1 presenting organization, 2 service organizations*
Tampa: 1 theater group
Miami: 14 theater groups, 1 presenting organization, 2 service organizations

Tampa. Twenty to thirty percent of Tampa's population have Spanish surnames dating back to the 19th century when Cuban cigar manufacturers and their employees settled in Tampa. Their descendants are now totally assimilated. The Spanish Lyric Theatre, founded in 1959 by Rene J. Gonzalez, produces four musicals a year on a modest $95,000 budget. Its repertory includes *zarzuelas* and musical revues in Spanish and Broadway musicals in English.

Miami. The Hispanic community comprises 43 percent of Dade County's 1.9 million population. Of the 700,000 Hispanics who live in Dade County, 60 percent have come to Miami from Cuba since 1959; most do not speak English. Sixty percent of Miami's population is now Hispanic. Miami's Hispanic theaters are all Cuban-run and all Spanish-language, reflecting the newness of the Cuban community and its close-knit population. They also reflect the community's isolation from Miami's non-Hispanic population and from other Hispanic groups in the United States. With few exceptions, the theaters operate only on earned income.

Latin countries do not have a tradition of private philanthropic giving, largely because their tax structures do not offer that incentive. That legacy, together with the Miami-Cuban community's isolation from the U.S. system of public and private arts contributions, has not made it easy for Miami-based Hispanic theaters to take advantage of available funding or to learn the techniques of running a not-for-profit arts organization.

An initiative to assist Hispanic theaters in Miami with organizational and funding information took place through the Metro-Dade Cultural Affairs Council in August 1984. Olga Garay-Ahern, now assistant director of the council, organized "Acting Together," a coalition of Hispanic theaters and independent producers to work together to seek funding. Participating theaters are Andromaca Players; Chicos, Inc. (a children's theater); Group of Associated Theatre Artists;

---

*Since the 1984-1985 survey was conducted, four theater groups and one service organization have closed, and four new theater groups have been established in Miami.

International Arts, Inc.; M.A.R.I.A.; Sociedad Pro Arte Grateli; Teatro Avante; Teatro Bellas Artes; and Teatro Prometeo.

This effort has been limited, however, by a 1980 Dade County Anti-Bilingualism Ordinance that prohibits the expenditure of county funds for any language other than English or any culture other than that of the United States. Federal and state funds, however, can still be channeled to Hispanic theaters through the Metro-Dade Cultural Affairs Council. The 1980 ordinance has been challenged and is now awaiting a hearing in Federal Court.

Apart from the commercial theaters run by Ernesto Capote, two theaters founded in the late 1960s survive on box office receipts and have annual budgets in excess of $200,000: Pro Arte Grateli, which produces ten to twelve *zarzuelas* each year, and Las Mascaras, whose two small theaters play farces like *Henriqueta se ha puesto a dieta* (*Betty Went on a Diet*) and *Vistete para que te respeten* (*Dress So You'll Be Respected*).

Teatro Avante and Teatro Prometeo, founded in the early 1970s, do more serious work, but on substantially smaller budgets. Avante lost its permanent theater space in 1983, and its director Mario Ernesto Sanchez has another full-time job. Prometeo, directed by Teresa Maria Rojas, is associated with Miami-Dade Community College. Both companies have begun to include English-language plays in their seasons.

Teatro Bellas Artes opened a charming 255-seat theatre in 1983. On an annual $150,000 budget, it produces or co-produces four plays a season, usually light comedies and translations of successful foreign plays. Chicos, Inc., one of three children's theaters in Miami, performs at Bellas Artes every Sunday morning, and Teatro Avante also uses the theater for its productions.

The Coconut Grove Playhouse's Hispanic program, initiated by Jose Ferrer in 1983, is now directed by Judith Delgado, a Puerto Rican who is the wife of the playhouse's current artistic director, Arnold Mittleman. They plan to include U.S.-Cuban and Latin American plays in future playhouse seasons.

WEST COAST (California, Washington)

Thirty-two theater organizations were surveyed on the West Coast: twenty-one theater groups; six presenting organizations; and five service organizations. All of the organizations are in California but one: The Group Theatre Company in Seattle.

Washington
Seattle: 1 theater group

The Group Theatre Company is a multi-ethnic, Equity organization directed by Ruben Sierra, who founded it in 1978. It operates out of a 197-seat house on the University of Washington campus. Sierra is paid by the university to run the theater, which is incorporated in its own right and functions autonomously. Originally from San Antonio, Texas, Sierra went to college in Seattle and stayed on to make it his home.

California: 20 theater groups, 6 presenting organizations, 5 service organizations*
Los Angeles: 8 theater groups, 1 presenting organization, 2 service organizations
Merced: 1 service organization
Oxnard: 1 theater group
Sacramento: 1 theater group, 1 presenting organization
San Diego: 2 theater groups, 1 presenting organization
San Francisco: 5 theater groups, 2 presenting organizations, 1 service organization
San Jose: 2 theater groups, 1 service organization
San Juan Bautista: 1 theater group
Santa Barbara: 1 presenting organization

Of the twenty theater groups surveyed in California, thirteen are Chicano-run; two are Mexican-run; one is multi-ethnic; and the remaining four are run by Hispanics of diverse backgrounds, mostly South American. Seven of these theater groups are continually active. They are El Teatro Campesino in San Juan Bautista; El Teatro de la Esperanza and the San Francisco Mime Troupe, which has become a multi-ethnic company and was managed by a Hispanic until 1986, in San Francisco; Bilingual Foundation of the Arts, ASCO, and Nosotros in Los Angeles; and Border Arts Workshop/Taller de Arte Fronterizo in San Diego.

---

*Since the 1984-1985 survey was conducted, two theater groups have closed, and one theater group and one presenting organization have been established in Los Angeles; one theater group has been added in San Diego; one theater group has closed in San Jose, one theater group has closed and one presenting organization has been added in San Francisco; one presenting organization has closed in Santa Barbara; and one theater group has been established in Costa Mesa.

The most active presenting organizations in California are the Galeria de la Raza in San Francisco, La Peña Cultural Center in Berkeley, Inner City Cultural Center in Los Angeles, and Centro Cultural de la Raza in San Diego. The Royal Chicano Airforce (Centro de Artistas Chicanos) in Sacramento presents dance performances on such religious and national holidays as *Cinco de Mayo, Dia de los Muertos* (All Souls Day), and *16 de Septiembre* and also teaches the techniques of mural painting. Its resident theater, Teatro de la Calle, closed in 1984. Four of California's six presenting organizations are Chicano-run; one is multi-ethnic; and one is diversified Hispanic with an emphasis on Chilean arts.

El Teatro Campesino and El Teatro de la Esperanza, founded in 1965 and 1969 respectively, are the strongest of the surviving teatros. As Luis Valdez pursued commercial success for his plays and as campesino members began to get jobs with other theaters, program activities in San Juan Bautista became sporadic and funding problems increased. In 1985, Valdez brought in Tony Curiel as an assistant director, which freed Valdez to write and to direct other projects. Among them have been his play *I Don't Have to Show You No Stinking Badges,* co-produced with the Los Angeles Theatre Center in 1986, and his film *La Bamba,* released nationwide in the summer of 1987. El Teatro Campesino is in the process of restructuring its organization to accommodate plans for future activities in San Juan Bautista and elsewhere.

El Teatro de la Esperanza is exploring ways to modify its collective structure and diversify its funding base. In the past, El Teatro has depended on touring for its primary income, but the heavy touring schedule necessary to maintain the company did not allow Esperanza to develop a home-base audience. In 1986 it moved from Santa Barbara to San Francisco where it can serve a large Hispanic population. With its longtime connection with Chicano and Latino theater, the San Francisco Mime Troupe serves some of this audience, but a larger Hispanic audience is more likely to respond to El Teatro de la Esperanza. The presence of Esperanza could also revitalize other Latino groups in the Bay Area, some of which do not now operate on a full-time schedule.

Two theater groups serve Los Angeles's 2 million Hispanics on a regular basis: Bilingual Foundation of the Arts (BFA), founded in 1973, and ASCO, founded in 1972. Under the direction of Carmen Zapata and Margarita Galban,

BFA is run as a professional Equity-waiver theater with a five-play season of works from Latin America and Spain, with a special interest in Garcia Lorca. For the past two years, BFA also been looking for U.S. Hispanic plays to produce. Plays at BFA are usually performed for a few weeks in English and then in Spanish; but sometimes they are done only in one language. The plays are selected to appeal to a wide audience—Hispanic community people, university students and faculty, and the general theater-going public. BFA's Spanish-language productions tend to attract larger audiences.

ASCO is composed of a group of Chicano visual artists and writers who stage one or two performance-art pieces a year in public spaces, art galleries, and universities. Their scripts include *Void and Vain* and *Success in Wearing the World's Largest Earrings*. In early 1987 they presented a work titled *Ismania* at the LACE Gallery. They are supported by commissions and performance fees and have built a large audience of artists and others interested in their nonconventional abstract style.

Nosotros, founded by Ricardo Montalban in 1970 to improve the image of Latino actors, has a small theater where it occasionally showcases plays or works-in-progress initiated by members. Each year it produces the Golden Eagle Awards program (the Hispanic version of the Academy Awards), which generates income to cover the organization's $180,000 annual budget. Nosotros also acts as an agency for Hispanic TV and film actors and publishes an annual directory of professional Hispanic actors. It is taking steps to strengthen its administration.

Inner City Cultural Center, one of the first minority arts organizations to be established in the 1960s, is located in a predominantly Hispanic neighborhood of Los Angeles. The center is multi-ethnic, with an emphasis on black culture. About one-third of the thirty plays presented there each year are Hispanic.

Plaza de la Raza, a strong community organization founded in 1971, has been going through a period of transition since the death in 1985 of Margo Albert, its artistic director and guiding force. Plaza has recently completed a 182-seat theater space dedicated to her memory. Plaza's primary contributions to the large Hispanic communities of Lincoln Heights in East Los Angeles where it is located, and adjacent Highland Park, are its classes in dance, theater, music, media, visual arts, and Mexican crafts. Students, most of whom are from the nearby communities, range from four-year-olds to senior citizens. The fees are nominal and can be waived if necessary. Theater classes in acting, dramatic readings, and production workshops are run by invited Hispanic playwrights and directors from the Los Angeles area.

Despite this activity, there is no Hispanic theater in Los Angeles responsive to the city's large Chicano or Central American population.[13] Several Chicano teatros have folded. The Mark Taper Forum has held several workshops on Central American themes during the past two years and is interested in continuing to produce Latino material, but it has not followed up in any significant way on its huge 1976 success with *Zoot Suit*. In October 1985 Jose Luis Valenzuela was hired to direct a Hispanic theater program at the Los Angeles Theatre Center (LATC), after several previous attempts to develop such a program had failed. Valenzuela is an experienced and talented director who has worked with El Teatro de la Esperanza and directed in Los Angeles on a free-lance basis. With Valenzuela, LATC now has an opportunity to create a serious Hispanic program.

La Galeria de la Raza, founded in 1969, is an active and respected art gallery in the heart of San Francisco's Mission District whose population is largely Hispanic. Rene Yañez, its former artistic director, incorporates performance-art pieces into the galeria's exhibition season. He also coaches young stand-up comics whom he presents in spaces throughout the Bay Area. The Mission Neighborhood Center, which occasionally presents local Hispanic theater groups, now houses El Teatro de la Esperanza.

La Peña Cultural Center has been active for twelve years and is still expanding. It now occupies three adjacent buildings in Berkeley, and will soon occupy nearly the entire block. La Peña was founded in 1975, two years after the military coup in Chile, by Chilean exiles and North Americans living in the Bay Area. It was named after the *peñas,* small cultural cabarets that sprang up in Chile in the late 1960s. La Peña presents 300 performing groups and serves over 200 community organizations, which use its facilities or its technical assistance each year. It also runs an art gallery, a restaurant, and a book and record store.

San Diego is a border town with Tijuana, Mexico. Much of the Hispanic theater activity there deals with border themes. The Centro Cultural de la Raza, founded in 1970 and located in San Diego's Balboa Park, is an active multi-arts center dedicated to border art in dance, theater, and visual arts.[14] It presents fifty performing arts events each year, most of them from California and Mexico.

Poyesis Genetica, a performance-art group founded in 1981 by Guillermo Gomez and Sara Jo Berman, was for six years the only consistently active theater group in San Diego; in 1987 the collaboration dissolved. Gomez has been instrumental in establishing a new organization, Border Arts Workshop/Taller de Arte Fronterizo, a collective that will continue to explore the relationship between Mexico and the United States through material with border themes. The workshop will produce live performances, and visual arts and video presentations at the Centro Cultural de la Raza.

Teatro Meta, directed by Raul Moncada, with William Virchis and Jorge Huerta acting as artistic advisors, is a Hispanic theater program of the Old Globe Theatre in San Diego. The idea for Teatro Meta, which emerged in 1980, was to offer training to actors of the San Diego Latino community and to produce Latin American and Hispanic plays. Its expanded program, which identifies Hispanic actors throughout the country to be considered for roles in Old Globe productions, is now in its second year. Teatro Meta recruits young Hispanic actors to participate in the Young Globe apprenticeship program and Hispanic directors and designers to work at the Old Globe. It plans to introduce Spanish classics and contemporary Hispanic plays into the Old Globe's repertory. Its program also includes educational and community training activities.

All of the California theater organizations mentioned above have budgets in excess of $100,000 with the exception of ASCO and Border Arts Workshop.

Teatro Nacional de Aztlan (TENAZ) was founded in 1971 to act as liaison for the many Chicano teatros that existed in California and the Southwest. It has sponsored biannual theater festivals since 1972. It holds periodic seminars to discuss the artistic goals, organization, and plays of member companies. It has also provided training workshops in acting, directing, writing, and creating a teatro. In 1981 it began publishing a newsletter, *TENAZ Talks Teatro*. With a declining membership, TENAZ is broadening its scope to include more theater groups and organizations and is also seeking more diverse funding.

Women in Teatro (WIT) was founded in 1978 to identify problems of Chicano women in theater, to institute within TENAZ a policy of upgrading the image of women and the roles they play on stage, to create support groups and child-care policies for women, and to establish open communications networks. WIT functions now more as an ideal than an organization. Carolina Flores and Elisa Gonzalez, who have been responsible for many of its accomplishments among the Chicano teatros, keep WIT goals alive at the TENAZ meetings and see that networking among women continues.

Of the twenty-three West Coast theater groups and presenting organizations with fact-sheet data, one has a budget in excess of $500,000; nine are budgeted between $100,000 and $499,999; one has a budget between $50,000 and $99,999; one between $25,000 and $49,999; two are budgeted between $10,000 and $24,999; and nine operate on annual budgets under $10,000.

SOUTHWEST (Texas, New Mexico, Arizona, Colorado)

Thirty-two theater organizations were surveyed in the Southwest: seventeen theater groups, ten presenting organizations, and five service organizations. Sixteen organizations are in Texas, six in Arizona, six in New Mexico, and four in Colorado. Twenty-five organizations are run by Mexican Americans.

> **Texas: 9 theater groups, 7 presenting organizations***
> Austin: 1 theater group, 1 presenting organization
> Del Rio: 1 theater group
> El Paso: 2 theater groups, 1 presenting organization
> Houston: 2 theater groups
> Kingsville: 1 theater group
> Mission: 1 presenting organization
> San Antonio: 2 theater groups, 4 presenting organizations

The Guadalupe Cultural Arts Center is the largest and youngest Hispanic arts organization in the Southwest. It is based in San Antonio whose population is more than 60 percent Hispanic. The Guadalupe Center was established in 1984 with a $479,000 grant from the city of San Antonio. Since that time, its budget has increased to almost $1 million. Housed in a renovated movie theater in El Barrio, it sponsors film and graphics programs and *conjunto* music festivals, and is the only

---

*Since the 1984-1985 survey was conducted, one theater group has been established in Dallas; one presenting organization has been established in Houston; one presenting organization has been closed, and one theater group has become active again in San Antonio.

Hispanic theater group in the city with an ongoing program of contemporary plays.[15]

The Carver Community Cultural Center, also in San Antonio, has presented some twenty-five different performing-arts events each season for the past ten years. The center has a strong focus on black performing and visual arts, but also includes Asian and Hispanic programs; the latter comprise about one-third of its season. Jo Long, the center's dynamic director, now cosponsors some of the Hispanic events with the Guadalupe Cultural Arts Center. Carver's audiences are diversified for all its programs.

The Centro Cultural Aztlan, founded in 1976, organizes cultural events around such holidays and anniversaries of historical events as *El Dia de los Muertos, Cinco de Mayo,* and the signing of the Guadalupe-Hidalgo Treaty. It publishes a bimonthly newsletter, and opened an art gallery in 1986. The organization is budgeted at $200,000.

The border town of Del Rio, due west of San Antonio, has an active and progressive community theater, Teatro Cultural del Pueblo, run by Diana Abrego. Its theater program, aimed at youth, deals with drugs, alcoholism, and machismo. It also has an arts-based counseling program.

Elenco Experimental, run by Argentine director Roberto Pomo at the University of Texas in El Paso, produces contemporary and classic plays from all over the world, including Spain and Latin America, as well as plays by U.S. Hispanics. Nicolas Kanellos, quoted several times in this report, runs Arte Publico Press at the University of Houston, an invaluable publishing outlet for contemporary U.S. Hispanic playwrights, poets, and fiction writers.

New Mexico: 3 theater groups, 1 presenting organization, 2 service organizations*
Albuquerque: 2 theater groups
Santa Fe: 1 theater group, 2 service organizations
Taos: 1 presenting organization

The distinctive cultural strains of New Mexico—Indian, Mexican, Spanish, and Anglo—are blended together in Hispanic arts. Hispanic theater activity in New Mexico is recent. The oldest theater organization, La Compañia de Teatro de

---

*Since the 1984-1985 survey was conducted, two service organizations have closed in Santa Fe; one theater group has been added in Taos.

Albuquerque, was founded in 1979; the more recent Teatro Aguacero in Albuquerque and Zona de Teatro in Santa Fe were established in 1983. La Compañia has an annual budget of $100,000 and an exceptionally active board of directors and fund-raising committee. Its artistic leadership, which has changed several times since 1979, is now under Irene Oliver Lewis. Ramon Flores, her immediate predecessor, is on leave of absence from La Compañia to participate in a directors program at Yale University's School of Drama. La Compañia has traditionally encouraged outside training for its artistic and technical staff. The organization's offices are located at Albuquerque's landmark Kimo Theatre. It produces one play at the Kimo each year; the remainder of its season of classic, contemporary, and new plays is presented at the smaller 350-seat Menaul Theatre, which was equipped with lighting and sound equipment in 1986.

Teatro Aguacero is a small, well-run community theater. Its original material is political in content. Some pieces are short skits with a single intention; others are more complex reflections of Mexican/Chicano life with folk, musical, and political elements. The energy of its director and playwright, Nita Luna, is reflected in the theater's work.

Zona de Teatro is a loosely structured company of six performing and visual artists in Santa Fe. They perform original plays or conceptual art pieces each year in such nontraditional spaces as churches, balconies of public buildings, and parks.

Suzanne Jamison, through the Santa Fe Arts Council, was particularly encouraging to alternative artists in Santa Fe. She resigned from the council in 1985, but continues to support theater groups and visual artists in the area.

Hembras de Colores, a presenting organization in Taos, was founded in 1981 by Enriqueta Vasquez. It is run by five performing and visual artists who organize cultural events around the annual celebrations of *Cinco de Mayo* and *Dia de los Muertos*. Vasquez often works on theater pieces with women farmworkers in the Taos area. Topo Rojo, a theater group founded in Taos in 1984, performs two to three plays a year for one or two weekend runs.

Arizona: 2 theater groups, 2 presenting organizations, 2 service organizations*
Phoenix: 1 presenting organization, 2 service organizations
Tucson: 2 theater groups, 1 presenting organization

*Since the 1984-1985 survey was conducted, one new theater group has been established in Tucson.

Hispanic theater activity in Arizona is young and concentrated in Tucson. Tucson has a larger Hispanic population than Phoenix, is closer to the Mexican border, and is heavily influenced by Mexican culture. El Teatro Chicano and Borderlands Theatre/Teatro Fronterizo were established in 1981 and 1984 respectively by former members of Teatro Libertad, a twelve-year-old teatro collective whose activities have waned. Until its reorganization in early 1987, El Teatro Chicano developed and performed plays by Silviana Wood, one of its founders.[16] Operating on a $30,000 budget, El Teatro Chicano has increased its membership and is expanding its repertory to include Latin American and U.S. Hispanic plays. Borderlands Theatre, operating on a similar budget, was formed to present material dealing with border issues. It also produces contemporary Latin American plays and plans to include non-Hispanic work. Like El Teatro Chicano, it is dedicated to producing plays bilingually. All of El Teatro Chicano's plays are bilingually written or adapted. Borderlands Theatre, on the other hand, presents some of its work, especially the plays from Latin America, in Spanish for several performances and then in English. Teatro Carmen is a presenting organization run by leaders of the Tucson Latino community. With a $50,000 budget and no paid staff, it presents local, national, and international touring companies at least twice a year. Teatro Carmen also contributes small sums of money toward production costs of work by El Teatro Chicano and Borderlands Theatre.

The three arts organizations located in Phoenix specialize in music or visual arts. One of them, Ariztlan, a service organization, holds a regular acting workshop that it would like to develop into a theater group. In 1986 the Bilingual Review/Press moved its headquarters from New York State to Arizona State University in Tempe. With its new headquarters in the heart of the Southwest, it is in an excellent position to serve a solid constituency of Hispanic writers.

Colorado
Denver: 3 theater groups, 1 service organization

In Colorado, Hispanics are concentrated in the San Luis Valley near the New Mexico border and in the Denver metropolitan area. Denver's 200,000 Hispanics represent 13 percent of its population. Because the city's Hispanics are assimilated, it is difficult to build an audience around Hispanic culture in Denver. The

Chicano Humanities and Arts Council (CHAC), founded in 1978, is attempting to create more interest in Hispanic visual and performing arts. The organization also functions as an advocacy base, sponsoring arts programs to encourage high school dropouts—a serious problem among Hispanics nationwide—to return to school.

Denver's three teatros operate on a part-time basis with budgets under $5,000. Su Teatro dates to 1972 and, like the early teatros, is run as a collective. Each of its five members has a full-time outside job. Ahora Teatro Hispano, founded in 1980, is a women's theater group that produces one original play a year. Teatro de la Familia, founded in 1981, is a community-based theater group whose members are mental health workers employed by Southwest Denver Community Mental Health Center. The group uses teatro techniques as therapy for mental health patients. The plays relate to social and psychological problems encountered by Mexican Americans. The group tours in Colorado and New Mexico.

MIDWEST (Illinois, Minnesota)

Five theater organizations were surveyed in the Midwest: three theater groups, one presenting organization, and one service organization. Four of these organizations are in Chicago and one is in Minneapolis. Two are Chicano-run, two are run by South Americans, and one is a collective of people from diverse backgrounds.

Illinois
Chicago: 2 theater groups, 1 presenting organization, 1 service organization*

According to the 1980 census, Chicago's population is 14 percent Latino, or 422,063. Today, however, it is estimated that there are close to 700,000 Latinos in Chicago, of whom 70 percent are Mexican American and 15 percent Puerto Rican.

> Chicago is the dominant center for Latino settlement in the Midwest and ranks fourth in Latino population among the nation's urban centers. There are more Mexicans in Los Angeles, more Puerto Ricans in New York, and more Cubans in Miami; however, Chicago has large populations of each in proportions almost equal to the national average. There are also many Central and South Americans. Chicago, then has a diversity of Latino communities that is without equal.[17]

---

*Since the 1984-1985 survey was conducted, one theater group has closed and two theater groups have been established in Chicago.

The Latino Chicago Theatre, the oldest ongoing Hispanic theater in Chicago, was created in 1979 by the Victory Gardens Theatre with a $98,000 grant from CBS. At first, little came from this ambitious beginning. The small teatros that antedated the Latino Chicago Theatre closed soon thereafter and the Latino Chicago Theatre itself has changed artistic and managerial leadership several times since its artistic directors stepped down in 1984. Juan Ramirez, who had acted as artistic consultant to the theater for two years and had run his own theater group, became the new artistic director in 1986. Under Ramirez's leadership, with the support and encouragement of the League of Chicago Theatres and newly elected Hispanic city officials, Latino Chicago Theatre is moving forward. In early 1987 it acquired a city firehouse in Wicker Park, an upwardly mobile Polish and Hispanic neighborhood. The space is being renovated to house its 1988 productions. Ramirez, who works with professional Hispanic actors, is interested in producing plays that express the reality of the lives of Hispanics in Chicago, the majority of whom are Chicano, rather than Hispanic plays, per se. He will also continue to present visiting Hispanic theater groups from other parts of the country and from Mexico.

The New Age Hispanic-American Repertory Theatre Company was founded in 1986 by Panamanian Rolando A. Arroyo-Sucre to produce Latin American and U.S. Hispanic plays in English. It hopes soon to have two companies—one producing in English and the other in Spanish. Arroyo-Sucre teaches at St. Augustine College, which owns a former film studio that is being renovated into two theater spaces. The Repertory Theatre Company will have access to them for its productions.

Konojel Junan ("The People United"), a new theater collective, develops its own pieces, which it performs in Spanish or in English. A women's group headed by Peruvian director Carmen Aguilar is in an embryonic stage of development. The Opera Factory, founded in 1978 to present rarely performed chamber music, added a Spanish *zarzuela* to its repertory in 1986. Director Blanche Artis Lewis plans a *zarzuela* production each season.

Pablo Neruda Cultural Center, a presenting organization established in 1979, focuses on Chilean cultural events. It has branches in New York, Washington, D.C., Philadelphia, San Diego, San Francisco, Madison, and Minneapolis. Nery

Barrientos, director of the Chicago center, cites audience development among the Chicano community as a major goal. Now its audiences are predominantly non-Hispanic.

Minnesota
Minneapolis: 1 theater group

Hispanics, most of whom are Chicano, are the largest minority in Minneapolis/St. Paul, comprising 8 percent of the population. Minorities are scattered throughout the metropolitan area, but there is a large Hispanic community in West St. Paul, settled around Our Lady of Guadalupe Church. Teatro Latino de Minnesota, which now works out of a community center in a black neighborhood in Minneapolis, is looking for space in West St. Paul. The Teatro was formed in 1981 with encouragement from El Teatro de la Esperanza through a training program conducted by Rodrigo Duarte-Clark. In 1985 Clark returned to Minneapolis where he worked with the group to develop an original piece. Teatro Latino is the only Hispanic theater group serving the Minneapolis/St. Paul Latino community.

PUERTO RICO
San Juan: 17 theater groups, 4 presenting organizations*

Theater people in Puerto Rico tend to be isolated from Hispanic and non-Hispanic theater life in the United States. They know New York theater, on and off Broadway, but know less about Hispanic theater in the rest of the country. There is also limited knowledge of administrative structures and funding mechanisms of U.S. not-for-profit theater. Although theater groups in Puerto Rico are incorporated as not-for-profit arts organizations, only two have tax-exempt status: Opera de Cámara and El Nuevo Teatro Pobre de America.

Most theater organizations act as independent production companies that operate almost entirely from earned income. Three that have succeeded on box office receipts have annual operating budgets over $200,000 and produce three

---

*Since the 1984-1985 survey was conducted, one theater group and one presenting organization have closed, and one theater group has been established in San Juan.

plays a year: Producciones Candilejas, founded in 1970 by Juan Gonzalez; Nuestro Teatro, created in 1979 by Carlos Ferrari, who writes his company's material; and El Grupo Teatro 60, founded in 1963 and run by Idalia Perez Garay, who mainly produces new Puerto Rican plays. Nuestro Teatro has a 400-seat permanent theater. Since 1983, when Grupo Teatro del 60 bought the 500-seat Teatro Sylvia Rexach, it has had difficulty sustaining itself financially. In early 1987 the organization was forced to rescind ownership of the theater, but hopes to be able to repurchase it in the future. Opera de Cámara and Producciones Cisne, both budgeted at around $100,000, operate from earned and unearned income. Founded in 1977, Opera de Cámara has received funding from the National Endowment for the Arts (NEA), the Ford Foundation, the city of San Juan, and small local businesses. It is well-run and is growing each year. It generally produces three chamber operas each season, at least one of which is a children's show. Opera de Cámara has begun to produce new operas out of collaborative workshops with contemporary Puerto Rican composers and librettists. It tours its operas to universities and cultural centers throughout the island. It also engages in educational programs at elementary schools. Producciones Cisne, founded in 1963 by playwright Myrna Casas and actress Josie Perez, generally produces two plays a season. Cisne also has a touring program, which takes its productions throughout the island.

There are three important community-based theaters in San Juan, all of which operate on budgets of $10,000 or less: El Nuevo Teatro Pobre de America, Teatro El Gran Quince, and Producciones Flor de Cahillo.

The Ateneo Puertorriqueño, founded in 1876, is the oldest cultural organization on the island. Its theater program was established in 1951 by Jose Lacomba and playwright Rene Marques. The Ateneo's cultural programs include theater presentations, concerts, lectures, seminars, exhibitions, political seminars, and awards. Each year it sponsors a Puerto Rican theater festival. It has an extensive library and historical archive. Though government-sponsored, the Ateneo is an autonomous institution.

On the other hand, the Instituto de Cultura Puertorriqueña, founded in 1955 by the Puerto Rican government, is a politically responsive institution whose personnel changes with each new government. One of its functions is to allocate federal funds to Puerto Rican arts groups. Most of the NEA funding channeled through the institute, which acts as a state arts agency, goes to theater groups selected to participate in the institute's annual festival of Puerto Rican plays. The institute has assisted theater groups with small grants over the years, but it has not provided them with information about direct funding possibilities from the NEA and private sources. In 1986 the institute itself received, for the first time, funds from the Puerto Rican government, which should allow it more flexibility in assisting arts organizations and in establishing its own performing arts programs.

The Centro de Bellas Artes, a state arts center with five rehearsal halls and three theaters with seating capacities of 2000, 750, and 250, was inaugurated in San Juan in 1981. Local theater groups use its rehearsal spaces and often rent its 250-seat house for productions. In addition to this new facility, which produces some 380 performances each year, the city has six other permanent theater spaces, ranging from the small 150-seat theater of the Ateneo to the 1800-seat space at the University of Puerto Rico. Large and beautiful theaters have also been built by the government in the cities of Ponce and Mayaguez. They are used, for the most part, to present touring theater and dance companies from San Juan or from abroad. There is some sporadic local theater activity in both cities, but theater in Puerto Rico is concentrated in the capital.

In the spring of 1985 the Puerto Rico Community Foundation (PRCF) was established with initial funding of $5,425,000.[18] It hopes to encourage increased philanthropic giving to Puerto Rican organizations, especially by U.S. companies that receive large tax benefits for their island operations. Thus far, the foundation is emphasizing social, economic, and educational programs, but has also established a permanent arts fund to sponsor island-wide community arts projects.

NOTES

1. *The Village Voice,* June 10, 1984, p. 114.

2. *Ibid.,* p. 39.

3. *The New York Times,* September 3, 1985, p. 17.

4. *The New York Times,* August 19, 1985, p. 1.

5. Hispanics are concentrated in 9 states, which control 193—or 71 percent—of the 270 electoral votes needed to elect a president. However, with the exception of Florida where Cuban-Americans register and vote in large numbers, the percentage of U.S. Hispanics who vote is very low.

6. *The New York Times,* August 18, 1985, p. 16.

7. Interview with Valdez, 1984.

8. Updated information on theater organizations as of 1987 is reflected in the narrative text of this report and in the attached directory (Appendix A). Statistical data in Chapter IV and Appendix B reflect the original survey completed in 1985.

9. At the time the survey was done, the Don Quixote Experimental Theatre and the Bubbles Players were operating in New York. The Don Quixote still produces and performs in Manhattan. The Bubbles Players, whose base was in Queens, closed in 1986 after the death of its founder and artistic director Manuel Martinez.

10. Pregones is not included in the statistical figures at the end of this report, nor is it described in the text, because Pregones staff did not wish the organization to be included in the survey.

11. Camillo died in January 1988. J.J. Johnson, one of the early members of The Family, has taken over as artistic director of the organization.

12. Joseph Papp's interest in Hispanic theater goes back to his 1964 production of Garcia Lorca's *The Shoemaker's Prodigious Wife.* The following summer in Central Park, he produced *Macbeth* in Spanish and Pablo Neruda's translation of *Romeo and Juliet,* staged by the late Argentine director Osvaldo Riofrancos. Papp's New York Shakespeare Festival has sponsored various Hispanic programs at the Public Theatre since it opened in 1967.

13. It is estimated that more than 300,000 Central Americans now live in Los Angeles.

14. Border art refers to performing and visual arts whose content deals with U.S./Mexico border issues.

15. Several vaudevillian theaters whose tradition dates back to the 1920s are still active in San Antonio.

16. Wood writes full-length bilingual plays and short skits, all with a sociopolitical point of view and a keen sense of humor. At the end of 1986, she resigned from El Teatro Chicano to broaden the exposure of her plays.

17. *Latinos in Metropolitan Chicago: A Study of Housing and Employment,* Monograph 6. Chicago, Illinois: Latino Institute, 1983, p. 8.

18. The Ford Foundation contributed $2 million; the Carnegie Corporation and the MacArthur and Rockefeller foundations contributed $500,000 each; the Charles Stewart Mott Foundation contributed $125,000; and one island-based corporation and seven mainland companies with operations on the island contributed the rest.

5. Recommendations

Hispanic theater in the United States is highly diversified in artistic expression, cultural heritage, use of language, managerial expertise, and degrees of professionalism. Artistic focus, priorities, and taste differ greatly among the theaters surveyed. Nonetheless, they face challenges similar to those of almost every theater organization in the United States: exploring both artistic self-definitions and ways to raise funds for survival into the 21st century. It is not surprising, then, that the organizations surveyed had similar institutional goals: more active information-sharing and networking, more extensive playwright development, better artistic and administrative training, improved marketing and audience development techniques, and the establishment of touring circuits. Even the most established companies felt the need for greater organizational stability to provide a more solid foundation for artistic growth.

Information Sharing and Networking

Hispanic theater organizations are increasingly receptive to sharing ideas, knowledge, and expertise. The groups surveyed are eager to brainstorm common approaches to artistic growth and more effective advocacy. They want to learn more about each other and share information about common needs, new dramatic material, artistic and managerial talent, and available technical assistance and funding.

Playwright Development

Theater groups throughout the country expressed the need for new dramatic material. Sometimes a group is simply unaware of Hispanic plays and playwrights outside its immediate geographic area. But there is also a serious shortage of new plays. Chicano teatros relied for years on collective work for their material, but are now turning to scripted plays. Until new playwrights emerge, some theaters will continue to use and/or adapt contemporary Latin American plays and world classics.

Artistic and Administrative Training

Most Hispanic theater groups are small. Seventy-two percent of those surveyed operated with annual budgets under $100,000; 32 percent had budgets under $20,000. Only 4 percent operated with budgets in excess of $500,000. Outside of the New York and Los Angeles areas, there is little opportunity for training actors, directors, designers, and technicians to meet the needs expressed by the groups surveyed. In administration, technical assistance is needed in every area—planning, fund raising, fiscal administration, and building and working with a board of directors—even among the larger organizations.

Marketing and Audience Development

Building an appropriate audience has been uniformly difficult. The most efficiently run theaters average a 55 percent capacity for the year. (The figure would be lower if paying audiences alone were included.) There is a critical need to improve marketing skills, especially for developing target audiences both at the theater's home base and on tour. Fifty-three of the eighty-seven theater groups surveyed have their own theater spaces. Forty-five of the fifty-five spaces have a capacity of under 300. Still, it is difficult to fill them with paying audiences for 90 to 150 performances per season.

Development of Touring Techniques

Touring can provide a source of earned income for theater groups and a means of sharing artistic ideas and work. Some theaters that would like to tour, however, lack the managerial expertise or established circuits to do it successfully. Other theaters find that touring requires more time and effort than they can afford and still achieve artistic or economic success in their operations. (Thirty-five percent of the eighty-seven theaters surveyed tour their productions, generally locally or regionally.) For theaters currently touring and those interested in touring, there is a need to establish national and regional circuits and to include Hispanic theater offerings in existing non-Hispanic circuits.

Conclusion

Since this survey was conducted in 1984-1985, Hispanic theater has continued to demonstrate fluctuation and vitality. Several groups have undergone major changes in artistic leadership; others have grown substantially, both artistically and financially. Some groups have had to close their doors, but new groups continue to appear. National and regional meetings of Hispanic theater people have taken place and others are being planned. Playwright development is being actively encouraged and other needs are beginning to be dealt with. Hispanic artistic expression, in all its diversity, continues to make an important, living contribution to U.S. theater.

APPENDIX A
Directory—United States, District of Columbia, and Puerto Rico

ARIZONA

Phoenix

Presenting Organizations

Zulma Jimenez, Executive Director
XICAN-INDIO
P. O. Box 1242
Mesa, Arizona 85201
(602) 833-5875

Service Organizations

James Covarrubias
ARIZTLAN
7111 East 4th Street
Scottsdale, Arizona 85251
(602) 941-5813

Lennee Eller, Executive Director
MOVIMIENTO ARTISTICO
DEL RIO SALADO (MARS)
P. O. Box 20431
Phoenix, Arizona 85036
(602) 253-3541

Tucson

*Theater Groups/Producing
Organizations*

Barclay Goldsmith
BORDERLANDS THEATRE/
TEATRO FRONTERIZO
334 South 6th Avenue
Tucson, Arizona 85701
(602) 882-8607

Arturo Martinez
TEATRO CHICANO
334 South 6th Avenue
Tucson, Arizona 85701
(602) 882-8011

TEATRO LIBERTAD
P. O. Box 775
Tucson, Arizona 85702-0075
(602) 620-6353

Presenting Organizations

Silvia Contreras, President
TEATRO CARMEN
334 South 6th Avenue
Tucson, Arizona 85701
(602) 882-8011

CALIFORNIA

Costa Mesa

*Theater Groups/Producing
Organizations*

Jose Cruz Gonzalez
Director, Hispanic Playwrights Program
SOUTH COAST REPERTORY
655 Town Center Drive
Costa Mesa, California 92628
(714) 957-2600

Los Angeles

Theater Groups/Producing Organizations

Harry Gamboa
ASCO
P. O. Box 3481
Los Angeles, California 90051
(213) 268-9138

Carmen Zapata, Producing Director
Margarita Galban, Artistic Director
BILINGUAL FOUNDATION
OF THE ARTS, INC.
421 North Avenue 19
Los Angeles, California 90031
(213) 225-4044

Jose Luis Valenzuela
Director, Latino Actors Workshop
LOS ANGELES THEATRE CENTER
514 South Spring Street
Los Angeles, California 90013
(213) 627-6500

Miguel Delgado
MEXICAN DANCE THEATRE
2633 East 2nd Street
Los Angeles, California 90033
(213) 267-0140

Isabel Castro, Acting Director
PLAZA DE LA RAZA CULTURAL
CENTER FOR THE ARTS AND
EDUCATION
3540 North Mission Road
Los Angeles, California 90031
(213) 223-2475

Rose Portillo
SEEDS OF FIRE
957 Tularosa
Los Angeles, California 90027
(213) 667-1863
(213) 664-1898 (messages)

Rene Rodriguez, Artistic Director
Rosemary Soto, Managing Director
URBANO ENTERPRISES
4427 Richard Circle
Los Angeles, California 90032
(213) 227-8839

Presenting Organizations

C. Bernard Jackson, Executive Director
INNER CITY CULTURAL CENTER
1308 South New Hampshire Avenue
Los Angeles, California 90006
(213) 387-1161

Jorge Luis Rodriguez
JORGE NEGRETE
STUDIO THEATRE
3665 Whittier Blvd.
Los Angeles, California 90023
(213) 268-6401

Service Organizations

Rene Enriquez
NATIONAL HISPANIC ARTS
ENDOWMENT
P.O. Box 4128
North Hollywood, California 91607

Rick Castro, President
NOSOTROS, INC.
1314 North Wilton Place
Hollywood, California 90028
(213) 465-4167

Merced

Service Organizations

Madelyn Gracia
MEXICAN AMERICAN
CULTURAL COMMITTEE
3449 M Street
Merced, California 95348
(209) 723-3530

Oxnard

Theater Groups / Producing Organizations

Javier Gomez
TEATRO INLAKECH
632 West Guava
Oxnard, California 93003
(805) 486-7468

Sacramento

Theater Groups / Producing Organizations

Loretta Redoble
TEATRO ESPEJO
2813 17th Street
Sacramento, California 95820
(916) 731-5302

Presenting Organizations
Gina Montoya
ROYAL CHICANO AIRFORCE
2119 D Street
Sacramento, California 95816
(916) 446-6362

Resource People

Carolina Flores
6131 Shupe Drive, Suite 36
Citrus Heights, California 95621
(916) 726-3319

San Diego

Theater Groups / Producing Organizations

BORDER ARTS WORKSHOP/
TALLER DE ARTE FRONTERIZO
c/o Centro Cultural de la Raza
P. O. Box 8251
San Diego, California 92102
(619) 235-6135

Raul Moncada
TEATRO META
c/o Old Globe Theatre
P.O. Box 2171
San Diego, California 92112-2171
(619) 231-1941

Marcos Contreras
TEATRO MESTIZO
P.O. Box 8274
San Diego, California 92102
(619) 284-3522

Presenting Organizations

Veronica Enrique
David Avalos
CENTRO CULTURAL DE LA RAZA
P.O. Box 8251
San Diego, California 92102
(619) 235-6135

Resource People

Jorge Huerta
Department of Theater
B-044
UNIVERSITY OF CALIFORNIA
La Jolla, California 92093
(619) 534-3791
(619) 436-6018

William Virchis
Department of Theater
SOUTHWESTERN COLLEGE
1604 Dartmouth
Chula Vista, California 92010
(619) 421-6700, ext. 346
(619) 421-5616

San Francisco Area

*Theater Groups/Producing
Organizations*

Rene Yañez
FUSION THEATRE
380 San Jose, #3
San Francisco, California 94110
(415) 285-7815

Rodrigo Duarte-Clark
EL TEATRO DE LA ESPERANZA
P. O. Box 40578
San Francisco, California 94140-0578
(415) 695-1410

Patrick Osbon, Managing Director
SAN FRANCISCO MIME TROUPE
855 Treat Street
San Francisco, California 94110
(415) 285-1717

Carlos Baron
TEATRO LATINO OF
SAN FRANCISCO, INC.
19 Precita
San Francisco, California 94110
(415) 648-6987

Presenting Organizations

Enrique Chagoya, Interim
Artistic Director
Humberto Cintron
Administrative Director
GALERIA DE LA RAZA
2851 24th Street
San Francisco, California 94110
(415) 826-8009

Laura Ruiz
LA PEÑA CULTURAL CENTER
3105 Shattuck Avenue
Berkeley, California 94705
(415) 849-2572

Oscar Maciel
Juan Pablo Gutierrez
MISSION CULTURAL CENTER
2868 Mission Street
San Francisco, California 94110
(415) 821-1155

Service Organizations

TEATRO NACIONAL DE
AZTLAN, INC. (TENAZ)
c/o El Teatro de la Esperanza
1290 Potrero Avenue
San Francisco, California 94110
(415) 695-1410

San Jose

*Theater Groups/Producing
Organizations*

Elisa Gonzalez
TEATRO VISION
523 S. Locust Street
San Jose, California 95110
(408) 295-0656

Service Organizations

WOMEN IN TEATRO (WIT)
c/o Elisa Gonzalez
523 South Locust Street
San Jose, California 95110
(408) 295-0656

San Juan Bautista

*Theater Groups / Producing
Organizations*

Luis Valdez, Artistic Director
Phillip Esparza, Producer
EL TEATRO CAMPESINO, INC.
P.O. Box 1278
San Juan Bautista, California 95045
(408) 623-2444

Stanford

Resource People

Tomas Ibarra-Frausto
Department of Spanish & Portuguese
Building 260
STANFORD UNIVERSITY
Stanford, California 94305
(415) 723-4977

COLORADO

Denver

*Theater Groups / Producing
Organizations*

Gerry Kite
AHORA TEATRO HISPANO
1408 Elizabeth
Denver, Colorado 80206
(303) 333-1094

Tony Garcia
Rudy Bustos
SU TEATRO
4771 Vine
Denver, Colorado 80216
(303) 296-0219

Ramon del Castillo
TEATRO DE LA FAMILIA
75 Meade Street
Denver, Colorado 80219
(303) 934-6757

Service Organizations

Carmen Atilano
CHICANO HUMANITIES &
ARTS COUNCIL (CHAC)
P.O. Box 2512
Denver, Colorado 80201
(303) 477-7733

CONNECTICUT

New Haven

*Theater Groups / Presenting
Organizations*

Tulio Ossa, Artistic/Executive Director
UNITED THEATER OF THE
AMERICAS/TEATRO UNIDO
DE LAS AMERICAS
319 Peck Street, Suite 362L
New Haven, Connecticut 06513
(203) 562-6480

DISTRICT OF COLUMBIA

Washington, D.C.

*Theater Groups/Producing
Organizations*

Hugo Medrano
GALA HISPANIC
BILINGUAL THEATRE
P.O. Box 43209
Washington, D.C. 20010
(202) 234-7174

Pedro Aviles
TEATRO NUESTRO
1470 Irving Street, N.W.
Washington, D.C. 20010
(202) 387-7277

FLORIDA

Miami

*Theater Groups/Producing
Organizations*

Jordana Webster
ANDROMACA
5021 Fillmore
Hollywood, Florida 33021
(305) 620-4083

Ernesto Capote
CAPOTE ENTERPRISES, INC.
420 SW 8th Avenue
Miami, Florida 33130
(305) 545-7684

Marta Llovios
CHICOS, INC.
5055 NW 7th Street, Suite 301
Miami, Floria 33126
(305) 447-1412

Judith Delgado
Hispanic Program
COCONUT GROVE PLAYHOUSE
P.O. Box 616
Coconut Grove, Florida 33133
(305) 442-2662

Maria Julia Casanova
GROUP OF ASSOCIATED
THEATRE ARTISTS
1840 SW 29th Avenue
Miami, Florida 33145
(305) 871-6400

Salvador Ugarte & Alfonso Cremata
LAS MASCARAS
2833 NW 7th Street
Miami, Florida 33125
(305) 649-5301
(305) 642-0358

Maria Malgrat
M.A.R.I.A.
1900 West 54th Street, Suite 403
Hialeah, Florida 33012
(305) 822-4103

Pili de la Rosa
PRO ARTE GRATELI
1059 SW 27th Avenue
Miami, Florida 33135
(305) 642-6935

Teresa Maria Rojas
PROMETEO
Miami-Dade Community College
300 NE 2nd Avenue
Miami, Florida 33132
(305) 347-3263

Julio O'Farrill
INTERNATIONAL ARTS, INC.
6027 SW 30th Street
Miami, Florida 33155
(305) 661-1251

Mario Ernesto Sanchez
TEATRO AVANTE
220 Cypress Drive
Key Biscayne, Florida 33149
(305) 361-2224

Mirella Gonzalez
TEATRO BELLAS ARTES
2173 SW 8th Street
Miami, Florida 33135
(305) 325-0515

Pepe Carril
TEATRO GUIÑOL
1521 SW 17th Terrace
Miami, Florida 33145
(305) 858-3147

Rafael de Acha
TEATRO NUEVO
P. O. Box 65096
Miami, Florida 33265
(305) 595-4260

Presenting Organizations

Pablo Chao
KOUBEK CULTURAL CENTER
University of Miami
2705 SW 3rd Street
Miami, Florida 33135
(305) 649-6000

Service Organizations

Josefina Rubio
ACCA (Asociacion de Criticos
y Comentaristas de Arte, Inc.)
1660 SW 31st Avenue
Miami, Florida 33145
(305) 446-5795

Resource People

Olga Garay-Ahern
Neighborhood Arts Grants Program
DADE COUNTY COUNCIL
OF ARTS AND SCIENCES
111 NW 1st Street
Suite 625
Miami, Florida 33128
(305) 375-4634
(305) 375-5019 (direct line)

Rosita Abella
Reference Desk
UNIVERSITY OF MIAMI LIBRARY
Coral Gables, Florida 33143
(305) 284-4706

Tampa

*Theater Groups/Producing
Organizations*

Rene J. Gonzalez, Executive Director
SPANISH LYRIC THEATRE
1704 East 7th Avenue
Tampa, Florida 33605
(813) 223-7341

ILLINOIS

Chicago

*Theater Groups/Producing
Organizations*

Julio Revolorio
KONOJEL JUNAN
1822 South Peoria
Chicago, Illinois 60608
(312) 421-2841

Juan Ramirez
LATINO CHICAGO THEATRE
1947 West North Avenue
Chicago, Illinois 60622
(312) 486-5120

Rolando A. Arroyo-Sucre
NEW AGE HISPANIC-AMERICAN
REPERTORY THEATRE COMPANY
1444 West Lunt
Chicago, Illinois 60626
(312) 465-8198

Presenting Organizations

Nery Barrientos, Director
PABLO NERUDA CULTURAL
CENTER
53 West Jackson Boulevard
Suite 631
Chicago, Illinois 60604
(312) 922-7240

Service Organizations

Jose G. Gonzalez, Director
MIRA, INC.
1900 South Carpenter Street
Chicago, Illinois 60608
(312) 829-1620

Resource People

Marta Ayala
MAYOR'S ADVISORY COMMISSION
ON LATINO AFFAIRS
City Hall, Room 703
121 North LaSalle Street
Chicago, Illinois 60602
(312) 744-4404

Victor Sorrel, Chairperson
Arts Department
CHICAGO STATE UNIVERSITY
B-600
95th and Martin Luther King Drive
Chicago, Illinois 60628
(312) 995-3984

MINNESOTA

Minneapolis

*Theater Groups/Producing
Organizations*

Ana Maria Mendez
Virginia McFerran
TEATRO LATINO DE MINNESOTA
3501 Chicago Avenue South
Minneapolis, Minnesota 55407
(612) 824-0708
(612) 546-1962

NEW MEXICO

Albuquerque

*Theater Groups/Producing
Organizations*

Irene Oliver-Lewis
LA COMPAÑIA DE TEATRO
DE ALBUQUERQUE
P.O. Box 884
Albuquerque, New Mexico 87103
(505) 242-7929

Nita Luna
TEATRO AGUACERO
1047 Atrisco
Albuquerque, New Mexico 87105
(505) 243-2090

Santa Fe

*Theater Groups/Producing
Organizations*

Elena Parres
ZONA DE TEATRO
468 West San Francisco
Santa Fe, New Mexico 87501
(505) 989-8036

Resource People

Suzanne Jamison
1807 Quapaw
Santa Fe, New Mexico 87501
(505) 983-2502

Taos

*Theater Groups/Producing
Organizations*

Rafael Guerrero
TOPO ROJO
P. O. Box 25
Los Cordobas Route
Taos, New Mexico 87571
(505) 758-1405 (messages)

Presenting Organizations

Juanita Jaramillo
HEMBRAS DE COLORES
P.O. Box 4388
Taos, New Mexico 87571
(505) 758-2789

NEW YORK

New York City

*Theater Groups/Producing
Organizations*

Sandra Maria Estevez
Executive Director
AFRICAN CARIBBEAN
POETRY THEATRE
1244 Grant Avenue, Suite 1C
Bronx, New York 10456
(212) 733-2150

Samuel Barton, Artistic Director
AMISTAD WORLD THEATRE
P.O. Box 249, Times Square Station
New York, New York 10108
(212) 662-9400

Carlos Garcia, Executive Director
CHARAS, INC.
605 East 9th Street
New York, New York 10009
(212) 982-0627

Osvaldo Pradere, Artistic Director
DON QUIJOTE EXPERIMENTAL
CHILDREN'S THEATRE
P.O. Box 112
Times Square Station
New York, New York 10108
(212) 244-5372

J. J. Johnson, Artistic Director
THE FAMILY REPERTORY
COMPANY, INC.
9 Second Avenue
New York, New York 10002
(212) 477-2522

GRUPO CULTURAL ORIENTACION
c/o Agustin Fortunado
514 West 184th Street, Apt. 42
New York, New York 10033
(212) 927-0053

Abdon Villamizar
IATI - INSTITUTO DE ARTE
TEATRAL INTERNACIONAL
9 East 16th Street
New York, New York 10003
(212) 242-9861
(212) 431-3613

Max Ferra, Artistic Director
Dennis Ferguson-Acosta
Managing Director
INTAR-INTERNATIONAL
ARTS RELATIONS, INC.
420 West 42nd Street
New York, New York 10036
(212) 695-6134

Victor Acosta/Mario Peña
Artistic Directors
Margarita Toirac, Executive Director
LATIN AMERICAN THEATRE
ENSEMBLE/EL PORTON (LATE)
P.O. Box 1259
Radio City Station
New York, New York 10101
(212) 246-7478

Nelson Tamayo, Artistic Director
Marta Garcia, Managing Director
LATEA (LATIN AMERICAN
THEATRE EXPERIMENT
ASSOCIATION)
107 Suffolk Street
New York, New York 10002
(212) 529-1948

Pedro Pietri
LATIN INSOMNIACS
400 West 43rd Street, Apt. 38E
New York, New York 10036
(212) 594-9835

Carla Pinza, Director
LATINO PLAYWRIGHTS
READING WORKSHOP
SERIES, INC.
267 West 89th Street
New York, New York 10024
(212) 724-7059

Eduardo Figueroa, Director
NEW FEDERAL THEATRE
LATINO WORKSHOP
466 Grand Street
New York, New York 10022
(212) 598-0400

Miguel Algarin
NUYORICAN POETS CAFE
P. O. Box 20794
Tompkins Square Park Station
New York, New York 10009
(212) 681-0169

Vera Colorado
OFF THE BEATEN PATH
P.O. Box 59, Prince Street Station
New York, New York 10012
(212) 431-1666

Pedro Monge
OLLANTAY CENTER
FOR THE ARTS
P.O. Box 636
Jackson Heights, New York 11372
(718) 565-6499

Rosalba Rolon, Executive Director
PREGONES, TOURING
PUERTO RICAN
THEATER COLLECTION
295 St. Ann's Avenue
Bronx, New York 10454
(212) 585-1202

Lourdes Ayala, Artistic Director
PROMETEO
c/o Ayala
86-34 St. James Avenue
Elmhurst, New York 11373
(718) 592-8310

Miriam Colon Edgar
Executive Artistic Director
PUERTO RICAN
TRAVELING THEATRE
141 West 94th Street
New York, New York 10025
(212) 354-1293

Gilberto Zaldivar, Executive Director
Rene Buch, Artistic Director
REPERTORIO ESPAÑOL
138 East 27th Street
New York, New York 10016
(212) 889-2850

Manuel Martin, Executive Director
TEATRO DUO
P.O. Box 1200, Cooper Station
New York, New York 10276
(212) 598-4320

Silvia Brito, Executive Director
THALIA SPANISH THEATRE, INC.
41-17 Greenpoint Avenue
Sunnyside, New York 11104
(718) 729-3880

Pablo de la Torre
TUTTI-FRUTTI COMPANY
115 Henry Street, Apt. 3C
Brooklyn, New York 11201
(718) 852-5899

Frida Castro
TYPICAL THEATRE OF BROOKLYN
112 Wyckoff Avenue
Brooklyn, New York 11327
(718) 366-1390

Alberto Minero
Director, Theatre Program
THE AMERICAS SOCIETY
680 Park Avenue
New York, New York 10021
(212) 249-8950

Oscar Ciccone
Cecilia Vega
Co-Directors
FESTIVAL LATINO
IN NEW YORK
The New York Shakespeare Festival
425 Lafayette Street
New York, New York 10003
(212) 598-7182

Nelson Landrieu
Nelson Tamayo
Mateo Gomez
RINCON TAINO
107 Suffolk Street
New York, New York 10002
(212) 529-1948

Bernardo Palombo, Director
TALLER LATINOAMERICANO
63 East 2nd Street
New York, New York 10003
(212) 777-2250

Presenting Organizations

Peter Bloch, President
ASSOCIATION FOR
PUERTO RICAN-HISPANIC
CULTURE, INC.
83 Park Terrace West
New York, New York 10034
(212) 942-2338

William Nieves, Director
EL CANEY DEL BARRIO
170 East 116th Street
2nd Floor
New York, New York 10029
(212) 534-9555

Service Organizations

Beatriz J. Risk
ASOCIACION DE TRABAJADORES
E INVESTIGACIONES DEL
NUEVO TEATRO (ATINT)
P.O. Box 1792, FDR Station
New York, New York 10150
(212) 752-0157

Jane Delgado, Executive Director
ASSOCIATION OF HISPANIC
ARTS (AHA)
200 East 87th Street, 2nd Floor
New York, New York 10028
(212) 369-7054

Roberto Maurano, Director
HISPANIC DRAMA STUDIO, INC.
804 Broadway
Brooklyn, New York 11206
(718) 384-4708

Carlos Carrasco, Artistic Director
HISPANIC ORGANIZATION
OF LATIN ACTORS (HOLA)
250 West 65th Street
New York, New York 10023
(212) 595-8286

TEXAS

Austin

*Theater Groups/Producing
Organizations*

Tomas Salas
LA PEÑA
225 Congress Avenue, Suite 256
Austin, Texas 78701
(512) 462-9052

Presenting Organizations

Hortencia Palomares
LEAGUE OF UNITED
CHICANO ARTISTS (LUCHA)
1402 East 1st
Austin, Texas 78702
(512) 477-5770
(512) 477-3364

Dallas

*Theater Groups/Producing
Organizations*

Cora Cardona, Artistic Director
TEATRO HISPANO DE DALLAS
222 South Montclair
Dallas, Texas 75208
(214) 948-6108

Del Rio

*Theater Groups/Producing
Organizations*

Diana Abrego, Director
TEATRO CULTURAL DEL PUEBLO
P.O. Box 964
Del Rio, Texas 78840
(512) 774-7201

El Paso

*Theater Groups/Producing
Organizations*

Roberto D. Pomo
ELENCO EXPERIMENTAL
Department of Drama and Speech
UNIVERSITY OF TEXAS
El Paso, Texas 79968-0549
(915) 747-5515
(915) 747-5146

Craig Kolkebeck
TEATRO LOS POBRES
c/o THE SOUTHWEST
REPERTORY ORGANIZATION
1301 Texas Avenue
El Paso, Texas 79901
(915) 533-1671

Presenting Organizations

Franklin G. Smith, Superintendent
CHAMIZAL NATIONAL
MEMORIAL
P.O. Box 722
El Paso, Texas 79944
(915) 534-6277

Houston

Theater Groups/Producing Organizations

Elsa Zambosco
MULTICULTURAL THEATRE
CORPORATION
5150 Hidalgo, Suite 1303
Houston, Texas 77056
(713) 621-3245
(713) 661-5971

Richard Reyes, Director
TEATRO BILINGUE DE HOUSTON
Ripley House
4401 Lovejoy
Houston, Texas 77003
(713) 921-5093

Presenting Organizations

Daniel Bustamante
FESTIVAL CHICANO
P. O. Box 3493
Houston, Texas 77001
(713) 673-2783

Resource People

Nicolas Kanellos
ARTE PUBLICO PRESS
University of Houston
Central Campus
4800 Calhoun Street
Houston, Texas 77004
(713) 749-4768

Kingsville

Theater Groups/Producing Organizations

Joe Rosenberg
BILINGUAL THEATRE
AMERICANA OF KINGSVILLE
1719 Santa Maria
Kingsville, Texas 78363
(512) 592-0753

Laredo

Resource People

Carlos Morton
Drama Department
LAREDO JUNIOR COLLEGE
Laredo, Texas 78040
(512) 724-6634

Mission

Presenting Organizations

Javier Gorena
XOCHIL ART CENTER
P.O. Box 373
Mission, Texas 78572
(512) 585-1761

San Antonio

Theater Groups/Producing Organizations

Pedro Rodriguez, Executive Director
Eduardo Diaz, Theater Manager
Jorge Piña, Director of Theater Program
GUADALUPE CULTURAL
ARTS CENTER
1300 Guadalupe Street
San Antonio, Texas 78207
(512) 271-3153

Sister Maria Carolina Flores, Director
TERCER ACTO
Our Lady of the Lake University
3726 West Durango
San Antonio, Texas 78207
(512) 434-6711 x-446
(512) 433-7771

Larry Garcia
TOVIAH THEATRE
428 East Myrtle
San Antonio, Texas 78212
(512) 224-8307

Presenting Organizations

Jo Long
CARVER COMMUNITY
CULTURAL CENTER
226 North Hackberry
San Antonio, Texas 78202
(512) 299-7211

Ramon Vasquez y Sanchez
CENTRO CULTURAL AZTLAN
211 South Pecos, Suite 239
San Antonio, Texas 78207
(512) 227-2751

Mary Ann Bruni, Director
FESTIVAL CALDERON
c/o TEXARTS, INC.
338 Park Drive
San Antonio, Texas 78212
(512) 826-2889

Resource People

Louis LeRoy, Executive Director
ARTS COUNCIL OF SAN ANTONIO
227 South Presa
San Antonio, Texas 78205
(512) 224-5532

WASHINGTON

Seattle

*Theater Groups/Producing
Organizations*

Ruben Sierra
THE GROUP THEATRE COMPANY
In Residence at the
Ethnic Cultural Theatre
University of Washington
3940 Brooklyn Avenue, NE
Seattle, Washington 98105
(206) 545-4969

Resource People

Yvonne Yarbro-Bejarano
Romance Languages GN-60
University of Washington
Seattle, Washington 98195
(206) 789-5343
(206) 543-2086

PUERTO RICO

*Theater Groups/Producing
Organizations*

Ernesto Concepcion
BOHIO PUERTORRIQUEÑO
Calle Verderon 959
Country Club
Rio Piedras, Puerto Rico 00924
(809) 769-3496

Pedro Santaliz
EL NUEVO TEATRO
POBRE DE AMERICA
Calle Dr. Stahl 207
Baldrich
Hato Rey, Puerto Rico 00903
(809) 751-7924

Maritza Perez
GRUPO PISOTON, INC.
Sol 316
San Juan, Puerto Rico 00901
(809) 724-3692

Idalia Perez Garay
GRUPO TEATRO DEL 60
c/o Drama Department
Humanities Faculty
University of Puerto Rico
Rio Piedras, Puerto Rico 00936
(809) 764-0000, ext. 2089

Teresa Marichal
LOS NUEVOS ALQUEMISTAS
P. O. Box 3773
Hato Rey, Puerto Rico 00919
(809) 766-0505

Carlos Ferrari
Eduardo Diaz
NUESTRO TEATRO
Minillas Station 40620
Santurce, Puerto Rico 00940
(809) 725-8011

Joset Exposito
NUEVO COLLAGE, INC.
Gales 2H24, Villa del Rey
Caguas, Puerto Rico 00625
(809) 743-9661

Luis Pereira
OPERA DE CAMARA, INC.
Edificio Gonzalez Padin
Local 504
Viejo San Juan, Puerto Rico 00901
(809) 723-3337

Carmen Gutierrez
PRODUCCIONES ACTORES
UNIDOS, INC
P.O. Box 6045
San Juan, Puerto Rico 00902
(809) 764-1543

Juan Gonzalez
PRODUCCIONES CANDILEJAS, INC.
P.O. Box 8166
Fernandez Juncos Station
San Juan, Puerto Rico 00910
(809) 724-7357

Carlos Canales
PRODUCCIONES CEIBA
P.O. Box 20769
Rio Piedras, Puerto Rico 00928
(809) 757-2629

Myrna Casas
PRODUCCIONES CISNE, INC.
Cond. Palma Real 5G
Miramar, Puerto Rico 00907
(809) 728-0928
(809) 724-1555

Zora Moreno
PRODUCCIONES FLOR
DE CAHILLO, INC.
Ave. Ramon B. Lopez 31
Rio Piedras, Puerto Rico 00923
(809) 758-5684

Luis Oliva
TEATRO CIRCOLO, INC.
P. O. Box 3612
Old San Juan Station
San Juan, Puerto Rico 00901
(809) 765-2754

Ramon A. Conde
TEATRO EL GRAN QUINCE
Calle 112 - BG19
Jardines de Country Club
Carolina, Puerto Rico 00630

Presenting Organizations

Jose M. Lacomba
Director, Theatre Program
ATENEO PUERTORRIQUEÑO
San Juan, Puerto Rico 00901
(809) 722-4839
(809) 764-6686

Carmen Junco
Gerente General
CENTRO DE BELLAS ARTES
Apartado 41227
Minillas Station
Santurce, Puerto Rico 00940
(809) 724-4747

Victoria Espinoza
Director, Theatre Program
INSTITUTO DE CULTURA
PUERTORRIQUEÑA
Calle San Francisco 305
San Juan, Puerto Rico 00905
(809) 724-0910

Resource People

Francisco Arrivi
Calle Pacific 14
Santurce, Puerto Rico 00911
(809) 728-7907

Rosa L. Marquez
140 B (Ed. 190)
El Monte Sur
Hato Rey, Puerto Rico 77901
(809) 765-5126

Appendix B
U.S. Hispanic Theater Survey Data, 1985

GEOGRAPHICAL LOCATION

	Total	(FS)	Theater Groups	(FS)	Presenters	(FS)	Service Orgs.	(FS)
WEST COAST[1]								
California	31	(27)	20	(18)	6	(5)	5	(4)
Washington	1	(1)	1	(1)	0		0	
	32	(28)	21	(19)	6	(5)	5	(4)
SOUTHWEST[2]								
Arizona	6	(5)	2	(2)	2	(2)	2	(1)
Colorado	4	(4)	3	(3)	0		1	(1)
New Mexico	6	(6)	3	(3)	1	(1)	2	(2)
Texas	16	(14)	9	(9)	7	(5)	0	
	32	(29)	17	(17)	10	(8)	5	(4)
MIDWEST[3]								
Illinois	4	(2)	2	(1)	1	(1)	1	(0)
Minnesota	1	(1)	1	(1)	0		0	
	5	(3)	3	(2)	1	(1)	1	(0)
EAST COAST[4]								
Connecticut	1	(1)	1	(1)	0		0	
District of Columbia	2	(2)	2	(2)	0		0	
New York	34	(24)	25	(18)	6	(5)	3	(1)
Florida	18	(14)	15	(13)	1	(0)	2	(1)
	55	(41)	43	(34)	7	(5)	5	(2)
PUERTO RICO								
(San Juan)[5]	21	(19)	17	(15)	4	(4)	0	
TOTAL	145	(120)	101	(87)	28	(23)	16	(10)

Note: Figures in parentheses represent the number of organizations for which Fact Sheets (FS) were filled out at the time of the 1984-1985 survey and data for which are included on the following pages.

YEARS ESTABLISHED

	Total	Theater Groups	Presenters	Service Orgs.
1 - 5 Years	41	30	8	3
6 - 10 years	34	23	6	5
11 - 19 years	34	27	5	2
Over 20 years	11	7	4	0
TOTAL	120	87	23	10

INCORPORATED

	Total	Theater Groups	Presenters	Service Orgs.
Yes	98	74	16	8
No	16	12	2	2
Government Affiliated	6	1	5	0
TOTAL	120	87	23	10

TAX EXEMPT

	Total	Theater Groups	Presenters	Service Orgs.
Yes	70	49	14	7
No	44	37	4	3
Government Affiliated	6	1	5	0
TOTAL	120	87	23	10

BOARD OF DIRECTORS

	Total	Theater Groups	Presenters	Service Orgs.
0 - 3	30	23	5	2
4 - 9	62	47	11	4
10 - 19	19	13	3	3
Over 20	9	4	4	1
TOTAL	120	87	23	10

PERMANENT THEATER SPACE

	Total	Theater Groups	Presenters	Service Orgs.
Yes	69	53	16	0
No	51	34	7	10
TOTAL	120	87	23	10

CAPACITY OF HOUSE(S)

	Total	Theater Groups	Presenters	Service Orgs.
1 - 99	17	10	7	n/a
100 - 199	30	21	9	n/a
200 - 299	17	14	3	n/a
300 - 399	1	1	0	n/a
400 - 499	3	2	1	n/a
500 - 599	2	1	1	n/a
600 - 699	1	1	0	n/a
700 - 799	3	2	1	n/a
800 or more	6	3	3	n/a
Not applicable	51	34	7	10
TOTAL	131	89	32	10

NUMBER OF PLAYS/PERFORMANCE PIECES PRODUCED ANNUALLY

	Total	Theater Groups	Presenters	Service Orgs.
1	10	10	0	n/a
2	19	16	3	n/a
3	28	25	3	n/a
4	19	19	0	n/a
5	7	7	0	n/a
6	2	2	0	n/a
7 - 12	8	4	4	n/a
13 - 19	2	0	2	n/a
20 - 49	7	0	7	n/a
50 - 99	1	0	1	n/a
100 or more	3	0	3	n/a
Not applicable	14	4	0	10
TOTAL	120	87	23	10

EQUITY AFFILIATED

	Total	Theater Groups	Presenters	Service Orgs.
Yes	14	13	1	n/a
No	96	74	22	n/a
Not applicable	10	0	0	10
TOTAL	120	87	23	10

ACTORS PAID

	Total	Theater Groups	Presenters	Service Orgs.
Yes	82	63	19	n/a
No	14	13	1	n/a
Sometimes	9	6	3	n/a
Not applicable	15	5	0	10
TOTAL	120	87	23	10

ANNUAL ATTENDANCE

	Total	Theater Groups	Presenters	Service Orgs.
0 - 1,000	3	2	1	n/a
1,000 - 4,999	31	26	5	n/a
5,000 - 9,999	24	20	4	n/a
10,000 - 19,999	18	14	5	n/a
20,000 - 29,000	9	7	2	n/a
30,000 - 39,000	7	4	3	n/a
40,000 - 49,000	1	0	1	n/a
50,000 and over	10	8	2	n/a
Not applicable	17	7	0	10
TOTAL	120	87	23	10

OUTREACH ACTIVITIES

	Total	Theater Groups	Presenters	Service Orgs.
Classes/Workshops	65	48	10	7
School Performances	46	42	4	0
Touring Activity	34	31	3	0
Newsletter	6	0	2	4
Other	46	28	11	7
TOTAL	197	149	30	18

OPERATING BUDGET

	Total	Theater Groups	Presenters	Service Orgs.
0 - 999	1	0	1	0
1,000 - 4,999	11	8	1	2
5,000 - 9,999	14	13	1	0
10,000 - 19,999	12	11	0	1
20,000 - 29,999	7	5	2	0
30,000 - 39,999	5	3	1	1
40,000 - 49,999	7	4	3	0
50,000 - 59,999	3	2	0	1
60,000 - 99,999	18	14	2	2
100,000 - 199,999	15	9	5	1
200,000 - 299,999	11	7	4	0
300,000 - 499,999	6	4	1	1
500,000 or over	6	4	2	0
Not applicable	4	3	0	1
TOTAL	120	87	23	10

PAID STAFF

	Total	Theater Groups	Presenters	Service Orgs.
0	51	42	6	3
1	10	7	3	0
2	17	10	3	4
3	13	10	1	2
4	3	1	2	0
5	4	3	1	0
6	2	1	0	1
7	7	3	4	0
8	2	1	1	0
9	4	3	1	0
10	2	2	0	0
11 - 20	4	4	0	0
21 - 30	1	0	1	0
TOTAL	120	87	23	10

VOLUNTEERS

	Total	Theater Groups	Presenters	Service Orgs.
0	25	15	4	6
1 – 4	20	18	1	1
5 – 9	26	19	7	0
10 – 19	28	20	4	3
20 – 29	4	3	1	0
30 – 49	9	8	1	0
50 or more	8	4	4	0
TOTAL	120	87	23	10

FUNDING SOURCES

	Total	Theater Groups	Presenters	Service Orgs.
State/Local	75	51	17	7
National	51	34	11	6
Private/Foundations/ Corporations	73	51	14	8
Box Office/Commissions/ Performance Fees	110	84	23	3
None	3	3	0	0
TOTAL	312	223	65	24

NOTES

1. In California, those not included in the survey's statistical data were: two theater groups, Teatro Intimo in Los Angeles and Teatro Inlakech in Oxnard; one service organization, the Mexican American Cultural Commission in Merced; and one presenter, Casa de la Raza Cocina in Santa Barbara.

2. In Arizona, MARS, a service organization in Phoenix, was not included in the statistical data of the survey. In Texas, two presenting organizations, the Xochil Art Center in Mission and Festival Calderon in San Antonio, were not included.

3. In Chicago, the Royal Boulevard Theatre and MIRA, a service organization, were not included in the statistical data.

4. In New York, the theater groups not included in the survey's statistical data were Amistad Theatre, Arte Unido, the New Federal Theatre's Hispanic Workshop, Off the Beaten Path, Pregones, Prometeo, Typical Theatre of Brooklyn; one presenter, New York Shakespeare Festival's Festival Latino; and two service organizations, ATINT and Hispanic Drama Studio. In Florida, two theater groups, Capote Enterprises and Chicos, Inc.; one presenter, Koubek Cultural Center; and one service organization, ACCA, were not included.

5. In Puerto Rico, two theater groups, Bohio Puertorriqueño and Producciones Ceiba, were not included in the statistical data.